United States
Environmental Protection
Agency

PRP SEARCH BENCHMARKING AND REGIONAL PRACTICES EVALUATION

FINAL REPORT

U.S. Environmental Protection Agency
Office of Site Remediation Enforcement

September 2010

TABLE OF CONTENTS

Appendix A – Site Universe Data
Appendix B – Programmatic Questionnaire
Appendix C – Programmatic Questionnaire Responses

ACRONYMS

CER	Cost-efficiency ratio
CERCLA	Comprehensive Environmental Response, Compensation, and Liability Act
CERCLIS	Comprehensive Environmental Response, Compensation, and Liability Information System
CI	Civil investigator
CPD	Cost per determination
EC	Enforcement coordinator
EPA	U.S. Environmental Protection Agency
EPM	Enforcement project manager
FTE	Full-time equivalent
HRS	Hazard Ranking System
IFMS	Integrated Financial Management System
NPL	National Priorities List
OECA	Office of Enforcement and Compliance Assurance
ORC	Office of Regional Counsel
OSRE	Office of Site Remediation Enforcement
PA/SI	Preliminary assessment/site investigation
PRC	Program results code
PRP	Potentially responsible party
QA	Quality assurance
RA	Remedial action
RCRA	Resource Conservation and Recovery Act
RD/RA	Remedial design/remedial action
REPA	RCRA enforcement permitting assistance
RI/FS	Remedial investigation/feasibility study
ROD	Record of decision
RPM	Remedial project manager
ROI	Return on investment
SAA	Superfund alternative approach
SCORPIOS	Superfund Cost Recovery Package Imaging and On-Line System
SEE	Senior Environmental Employee
SF	Superfund
SNL	Special notice letter
SOP	Standard operating procedure

I. EXECUTIVE SUMMARY

In November 2003, Acting Deputy Administrator Stephen L. Johnson requested an internal review of the Superfund program (the "120-Day Study") to identify opportunities to achieve program efficiencies that would enable EPA to begin and complete more long-term cleanups with existing program resources. One of the recommendations resulting from that review was to evaluate regional PRP search programs to identify practices indicative of enforcement success and barriers to achieving it. In response to this recommendation, the Office of Site Remediation Enforcement (OSRE) undertook a PRP search evaluation in consultation with the National PRP Search Enhancement Team.

OSRE determined that the PRP search evaluation should focus on PRP searches at NPL and SAA sites with either a post-FY1999 PRP Search Completion date or a post-FY1999 Final RA Start date in CERCLIS. OSRE believed that this is the largest group of sites where extensive PRP searches were performed under uniform program guidance and data reporting requirements. The site universe includes both enforcement- and Fund-lead sites. In response to concerns voiced by members of the National PRP Search Enhancement Team that PRP searches might be considered ineffective or inefficient if regions concluded that there were no viable responsible parties at particular sites, OSRE decided that the evaluation criterion should be the actual determination of whether a party is a liable and/or viable PRP and not just the number of PRPs determined to be liable and viable. Thus a cost per PRP determination (CPD) indicator was used in this analysis.

Four main data points were used for benchmarking analyses: PRP determinations, PRP search costs, EPA response costs, and PRP response costs. OSRE relied primarily on IFMS data to determine total EPA response costs and PRP search costs and primarily on CERCLIS data for PRP determinations and PRP response costs. PRP search costs and EPA response costs include direct and estimated indirect costs. Each data point was updated during the study. Preliminary analysis indicated that site groups with the greatest variability in total search costs and CPD were owner/operator sites, waste contributor sites, and sites with de minimis parties. Data analysis therefore focused on these groups. In addition, OSRE surveyed EPA's regions to identify PRP search practices and barriers to effective and efficient PRP searches and to identify additional variables that might explain regional CPD differences.

Results of the data analysis and survey demonstrate that the uniqueness of each PRP search is the major challenge to evaluating the effectiveness and efficiency of search activities and to identifying PRP search practices and barriers to success. Even among sites categorized by type, each has unique characteristics that affect the conduct of the PRP search. Each PRP search presents its own obstacles and each regional program adapts its own unique practices and procedures to overcome them as they arise. This is an area that may require additional study in the future.

PRP search costs varied widely, both among sites and among regions. Median PRP search costs per site proved to be highest at de minimis sites and lowest at owner/operator sites, with waste contributor sites occupying the middle ground closer to the owner/operator median. While the owner/operator median was lowest compared to other groups, owner/operator sites showed the greatest variability in overall PRP search costs. This characteristic appears to be a result of the inclusion in this group of a small number of extensive mining and area-wide ground water sites with large numbers of owners. These sites had atypically large numbers of potential owner/operator parties, resulting in very high overall PRP search costs that are not typical of most owner/operator sites.

OSRE considered the possibility that costs might vary between searches conducted by EPA and those conducted by contractors. The study did not analyze this factor as a variable, however, because it did not clearly distinguish regions from each other. Survey responses indicated that regions generally try to perform as much search work as possible with intramural resources, but that all regions use contractors at least occasionally for search-related tasks. This is another area that may require additional study in the future. While OSRE considered evaluating factors other than site type, such as regional organization, survey responses did not provide sufficient information to group regions into discrete categories based on such factors.

CPD varied considerably less by site type than did total PRP search costs. Median CPD was highest at owner/operator sites and lowest at de minimis sites, with waste contributor sites occupying the middle ground closer to the de minimis median. This reversal of trends in PRP search costs indicates that economies of scale were at work; CPD tended to fall as either the number of determinations or total PRP search costs rose. This reversal and the overall reduction in CPD variability compared to PRP search costs generally held true at the regional level as well, indicating a high degree of consistency in regional search practices.

Return on investment (ROI), the dollar amount of PRP response and cost recovery commitments as compared to total PRP search costs, displayed the same pattern as CPD. Owner-operator sites showed the highest median ROI, de minimis sites the lowest, with waste contributor sites occupying the middle ground closer to the de minimis median. Sites with higher CPD generally had lower total PRP search costs and lower numbers of determinations. Sites with lower total PRP search costs generally had higher ROI. This relationship generally held true at the regional level, although ROI at owner/operator sites varied considerably and may warrant further investigation.

PRP search costs for all sites averaged approximately 6% of total EPA expenditures plus estimated future work performed by PRPs at those sites. This figure varied widely, from 1% at owner/operator sites to nearly 8% at waste contributor sites to over 19% at waste management sites.

In this study, EPA collected information on regional PRP search organizational and operational characteristics to determine if there was any correlation between the outcomes of the site-specific analyses and regional program characteristics. Responses to the survey were not sufficiently consistent to compare to site-specific data, but they provided certain insights into the operation of regional PRP search programs:

- Whether regions use separate organizational units for PRP search functions depends on the size of the region.

- Whether regions dedicate specific job classifications to PRP search functions depends on the size of the region.
- Regions organize site-specific case teams to perform PRP search functions.
- Most regions have contract vehicles in place to obtain extramural support in performing PRP search functions.
- Regions tend to use contractor support either for skilled research and technical tasks generally required on an ad hoc basis or on routine and less skilled clerical and data management tasks.
- Regions charge outlays for contractor support site-specifically and concentrate them on case development and legal and financial analysis.
- Regions charge FTEs allocated for PRP search-related tasks site-specifically and use them primarily for case development and legal analysis and documentation tasks.
- Regions allocate funds available for PRP search-related activities on the basis of site-specific factors.
- Regions develop site-specific plans for conducting PRP searches.
- Regions initiate PRP search activity, e.g., a deed search for the current owner, during the preliminary assessment/site investigation (PA/SI) stage or at the earliest appropriate time before the site is proposed for the NPL.

These insights are the basis for the conclusions and recommendations set forth in Section V.

II. BACKGROUND

In November 2003, EPA Acting Deputy Administrator Stephen L. Johnson requested that a small work group be established to conduct a relatively quick internal review (approximately 120 days) of the Superfund program. The main objective of the review was to identify opportunities for program efficiencies that would enable EPA to begin and complete more long-term cleanups (remedial actions or RAs) with current resources. The review was motivated by EPA's lack of adequate funding to begin remedial actions at all the sites currently ready for long-term cleanup. This backlog is largely the result of the Superfund program's maturity. More sites have progressed through the remedial investigation and feasibility study (RI/FS) phases to the more costly cleanup phase. These sites also include larger, more complex sites that require multiple remedies, further increasing demands on the program's limited resources.

The 120-Day Study was conducted by a team of EPA headquarters and regional staff with broad knowledge of and experience in the program. The team gathered data from Agency systems, *ad hoc* data requests, interviews with program managers and outside experts, and tailored questionnaires. The team made recommendations designed to improve immediate resource utilization and help the program function more efficiently in the long term. Among these was Recommendation 53:

> To continue to increase the percentage of PRP cleanups and take further pressure off appropriated funds, OECA should conduct responsible party search benchmarking to identify strong regional programs. This benchmarking should be combined with PRP search audits to identify ways to strengthen regional PRP search programs.[1]

To implement this recommendation, the 120-Day Study Action Plan directed the following action:

> OSRE will conduct a Program evaluation of Regional PRP search efforts to determine the relationship between enforcement success and PRP search expenditures and practices. Additional follow-up actions will be identified based on the outcome of this evaluation. As a component of the Program evaluation, OSRE will evaluate Regional trends, PRP search "best practices," and barriers to identifying PRPs early and getting them to perform RI/FSs.[2]

---

[1] *Superfund: Building on the Past, Looking to the Future.* Washington, D.C., April 22, 2004.

[2] *Superfund: Building on the Past, Looking to the Future. The 120-Day Study Action Plan.* Washington, D.C., February 2005.

III. PROJECT APPROACH

The Office of Site Remediation Enforcement (OSRE) commissioned a PRP search evaluation ("the study") that would develop "site-specific and programmatic measures to assess the effectiveness and efficiency" of regional PRP search efforts, define the "universe of sites/actions" for measuring effectiveness and efficiency, collect data, and analyze the measures for which data were available from EPA data sources. OSRE consulted regional PRP search personnel through the National PRP Search Enhancement Team at each stage of the development and implementation of the study.

A. Site Universe

Sites in the study universe included all NPL and SAA[3] sites as of the start of the study that had either (1) a post-FY1999 PRP Search Completion date in CERCLIS, or (2) no PRP Search Start or Completion date in CERCLIS, but a post-FY1999 Final RA Start date. While the 120-Day Study was not concerned solely with NPL/SAA sites, OSRE believed that these sites involved the most extensive search efforts in view of the expense and duration of the response actions they require. The universe of sites was restricted to those with post-FY99 actions to provide as large a universe as possible while ensuring that the searches were performed under uniform program and data reporting conventions and represented "current practice." OSRE believed that searches at sites with post-FY99 PRP search completions/RA starts were likely to have been substantially conducted after implementation of Superfund Administrative Reforms and adoption of CERCLIS 3 data elements. Both enforcement- and Fund-lead sites were included in the study universe as regions must conduct PRP searches before concluding that response action at a site will have to be Fund-lead. Although cost data were updated in the course of the study, the study universe remained unchanged. The results presented here therefore may not fully reflect regional practice and organization that may have changed over the last several years since the cost data were last updated.

Regions reviewed the sites included in the study universe, and recommended that some be deleted and others added. Sites were recommended for deletion because they were state-lead, no PRP search was performed, the search was initiated in the distant past, the search was performed by state or federal trustee agencies, and for other reasons. Sites were added mainly because the PRP search had only recently been completed or the final remedial action only recently started. OSRE accepted the regions' recommendations on deletions and additions unless the region failed to provide the number of determinations[4] for a site it proposed to add. In total, 24 sites were deleted from the universe and four were added, resulting in a final universe of 135 sites.

Sites in the study universe were categorized according to CERCLIS site type. They were not sub-categorized by CERCLIS site subtype as the number of subtypes is too large in relation to the number of sites in the study universe for subcategories to be statistically significant. The

---

[3] Superfund Alternative Approach (SAA) sites qualify for listing on the NPL but are not been listed because PRPs have entered into early SAA agreements with EPA to perform the site investigation or cleanup.

[4] Determinations are discussed below in "Measures Development."

study universe sites fell into the following site types: MI (mining); MP (manufacturing/processing/maintenance); MT (multiple); OT (other); RE (recycling); and WM (waste management). OSRE reassigned MT and OT sites to one of the other categories based on information about the sites obtained through on-line CERCLIS queries and regional site fact sheets. The majority of OT sites were assigned to a new site type for ground water plume sites (GW). This site type does not exist in CERCLIS but is clearly indicated by the characteristics of the OT sites assigned to it. Sites in the study universe are therefore categorized as GW, MI, MP, RE, or WM.

B.   Measures Development

Regional comments and concerns were the key element in deciding how best to measure the "effectiveness and efficiency" of PRP searches. The regions' major concern was that searches would be regarded as ineffective or inefficient if they determined that there were no viable responsible parties at a site. The following regional comment sets forth this concern in full:

> Where a PRP search has been done on a site and the conclusion reached was that there are no viable PRPs, I would maintain that the two questions to be asked relative to how well that search was conducted are: 1) Is that conclusion correct and properly documented?; and 2) Was that result reached in as efficient and economical manner as possible? If the answer to those questions is "yes", I think the conclusion has to be that the search was well done. I, and I expect everyone else who has conducted PRP searches, has had sites where viable PRPs were identified with minimal effort and little expenditure of resources. We have also had sites [where] no viable PRPs were identified despite a major effort. I don't think that it necessarily follows that in one case the search was well done and in the other, it wasn't.

The commenter quoted above urged that arriving at the correct conclusion should be the focus of evaluation, "whether that conclusion leads to viable PRPs that EPA can pursue or a well documented conclusion that there are no such PRPs."

In response to this concern, which was echoed in other comments, it was decided that the evaluation criterion should be the determination of whether a party associated with a site is or is not a viable responsible party. This unit should remove any potential penalty for investigating leads that do not result in identification of a liable and/or viable PRP. A proposed definition of "determination" was circulated to the regions. In response to comments on it, "determination" was adopted as the unit of analysis and a final definition was formulated as follows:

> "Determination: The PRP Search Team's conclusion that any single, specific party associated with a CERCLA site is or is not a liable and/or viable PRP."[5]

Adoption of "determination" as the unit of evaluation lends itself to development of a simple

---

[5] The expression "and/or" replaced "and" at the regions' request to avoid the implication that a determination requires that a party be found both liable and viable or neither.

measure applicable to sites of any type in any region where PRP search activity is undertaken. This is the cost per determination (CPD), which may also be thought of as a cost efficiency ratio (CER).

$$\text{CPD or CER} \quad = \quad \frac{\text{PRP search costs}}{\text{No. of determinations}}$$

CPD is a straightforward, unbiased measure that is (1) both site-specific and programmatic and (2) permits comparison of the effectiveness and efficiency of PRP search activities between and within regions and site types regardless of the outcome of the search.

C. **Data Collection**

There are four main data points that were used for the benchmarking analyses: PRP determinations, PRP search costs, EPA response costs, and PRP response costs. Each of the data points was updated during the study.

Data on PRP determinations were originally pulled from CERCLIS. At the time, only positive determinations, where a party was determined to be liable, were available at EPA headquarters. Since PRP determinations needed to include negative determinations (which include all parties evaluated whether or not they are found viable and liable) as well, regions were asked to complete Regional Data Reports specifying the number of determinations made at each of their sites. Where specific separate information on determinations were not provided, CERCLIS PRP data were used as a surrogate. For the final data pull, all determinations were available to headquarters.

Data on PRP search costs were originally obtained from IFMS. Enforcement outlays with activity codes NS (NPL RP Search), RP (Non-NPL PRP Search), HV (interviews) and LA (laboratory support) were used to determine PRP search costs. Costs coded RP at study universe sites were included on the theory that they were incurred and coded prior to listing on the NPL but otherwise were an integral part of the PRP search. PRP search costs under either code include both direct and indirect costs as SEE employees engaged in PRP search-related tasks are generally charged as an indirect cost. Interviews and laboratory support costs were included as it was felt that interviews are an integral part of the search process and that site-specific laboratory support associated with enforcement are analyses performed to associate particular parties' waste with the site. Adding costs associated with the last two activity codes did not substantially change total PRP search costs at any site.

Due to substantial difficulties and delays experienced in obtaining information from the Office of the Chief Financial Officer, the first update of PRP search costs was obtained from EPA's eFacts database. This database incorporates data from IFMS. Regions were asked to provide updates on search costs as part of the Regional Data Reports. Final search cost data were extracted from IFMS via SCORPIOS.

As with the PRP search costs, data on EPA response costs were originally obtained from IFMS, updated once using eFacts, and updated again using data pulled from SCORPIOS. Indirect rates were applied to determine EPA's total response costs. Since some response work has been or will be done by PRPs, or will be paid for by PRPs as future costs, settlement data were extracted from CERCLIS. The estimated value of work and federal future costs were added to EPA response costs to obtain total response costs for each site.

Data collection results are set forth in Appendix A.

D.   Data Quality Issues

Although the regions participated in developing and defining PRP "determination," it is a novel metric and the regions had to compute it for their sites without the benefit of prior experience, guidance, or standard procedures. As noted below, regions relied on a variety of sources to do so, raising the possibility that regions tabulated the number of determinations differently or that the quality or condition of site records affected their accuracy. The difficulties that some regions encountered computing the number of determinations, however, appear to have been related more to lack of resources to compile information than to availability of information.

Regions were asked to identify the sources of information they relied on for number of determinations when completing Regional Data Requests. Identified sources included site files, site documents, administrative records, settlement documents, CERCLA Section 104(e) letters, litigation referrals, depositions, de minimis offers, general and special notice letters, civil investigator memoranda, orphan share memoranda, pre-referral negotiation packages, site transactional records (i.e., manifests, drop tickets, invoices, and cancelled checks), title searches, waste-in allocations, volumetric ranking summaries, baseline PRP search reports, surveys, state records, manifests, receipts, and interviews with civil investigators (CIs), attorneys, contractors, case developers, remedial project managers (RPMs), enforcement project managers (EPMs), and enforcement coordinators (ECs). In other words, information on determinations was available, but not necessarily from one or the same sources, and some regions were able to make more resources available to locate and compile such information than others.

The Regional Data Request QA rounds clarified understanding of PRP determinations and also helped identify appropriate sources of information about them. In view of the number of updates received, the QA rounds succeeded in improving the quality of data about determinations, search costs, and cleanup costs. Regions were unable to provide determination figures for 18 sites. OSRE defaulted to the number of PRPs listed in CERCLIS for 15 of those sites. The number of determinations was assumed to be one at the other three sites, where CERCLIS indicated that there were no identified PRPs. This may sometimes be the actual number of determinations, but one would expect it to be larger in many cases. This limitation is likely to result in higher CPDs at some sites than would be the case if accurate determination figures were available.

Some regions observed that PRP search costs originally derived from dated IFMS data varied noticeably from their own figures, and suggested that this might be due to select logic using the LA code. Regions had the opportunity to submit corrected cost figures, however, and a number of them took advantage of it as discussed above in connection with data collection. The submitted data included search costs for 31 sites. In some cases, the data were close to the eFacts data, but in others they varied more than $100,000 higher or lower than the eFacts data.

This is likely because the search cost updates were sometimes based on different criteria. Of the three regions submitting them, one included only NS costs, one based its PRP search costs on its records of expenditures for the four activity codes specified by OSRE (RP, NS, HV, LA), and another added site-specific payroll costs for CIs to the PRP search costs contained in eFacts/IFMS.

Analysis of the eFacts data for the study sites showed that there were only 16 HV transactions and 96 LA transactions with an enforcement Program Responsibility Code (PRC) at 22 sites in the study, with no more than $29,200 (including indirect costs) at any one site. Only five of the sites had HV and LA costs greater than $10,000. Because of its insignificant impact, we chose to include the HV and LA costs in the analysis. These criteria were also used in the final pull of IFMS data from SCORPIOS.

Nevertheless, OSRE was concerned that regions were using different definitions of and methodologies for determining PRP search costs. In order to provide a consistent basis for the results, OSRE decided to rely on the IFMS data to determine total EPA response costs and PRP search costs using the PRCs and activity codes described earlier.

E.   Programmatic Survey

OSRE conducted a survey of EPA's regions to help it identify PRP search practices and barriers to effective and efficient PRP searches. The survey also sought to identify additional variables that might explain regional CPD differences.   The survey questionnaire was based on one developed for evaluation of the Superfund removal program. A copy of the questionnaire may be found in Appendix B. Survey responses were compiled, entered on a spreadsheet, and subjected to intensive content analysis. A summary may be found in Appendix C. Responses to the programmatic survey form the basis of the narrative set forth in Section IV.B below.

IV. RESULTS AND FINDINGS

Data collected from IFMS, Regional Data Reports, eFacts, and SCORPIOS, and the results of the programmatic survey make it clear that the uniqueness of each PRP search is the major challenge to evaluating the effectiveness and efficiency of search activities and identifying PRP search practices and barriers to success. Even among sites categorized by type, each has unique geography, geology, operations, availability of site records, and risk characteristics that impact the PRP search strategy. Each search presents its own obstacles and each regional program adapts its own unique practices and procedures to overcome them as they arise. The site study universe would have to be considerably larger than it is to permit meaningful analysis of any but a few of the variables that may account for the effectiveness and efficiency of PRP search activities.

A. Data Evaluation

Preliminary analysis of the data yielded several variables that had the most influence on total search costs and CPD. Several site types displayed enough variability to study. Of the site type groups, the largest were waste management (23 sites) and area-wide ground water (20 sites). The 135 sites included 36 owner/operator sites, 99 waste contributor sites, and 20 sites with de minimis parties.

PRP determinations, search costs, and cleanup costs were analyzed for all sites, including the groups named above. Due to issues in Region ██ related to site charging for PRP search costs, a decision was made to exclude their sites from this study. In collecting data from IFMS for Region ██ OSRE noticed that their PRP search costs were significantly lower than in other regions. In discussions with the regional PRP search manager it was determined that in-house CIs were directed to charge their time to the "negotiations" activity code even though they primarily conducted PRP searches. The rationale for this practice is unclear. As a result, it was difficult to identify what portion of the CIs' time was devoted to PRP searches and what portion to negotiations. Because most of the search work in Region ██ is conducted in house, this created a significant data quality problem relative to our analysis methodology that could not be easily resolved. Since this finding, OSRE has spoken with the region and understands that the region has corrected this charging issue prospectively but was unable to do so for historical data so as to enable OSRE to include it in the study.

1. PRP Search Costs

PRP search costs (including indirect costs) varied widely, with a median search cost of just under $75,000 for all sites in the sample. The median search cost for waste contributor sites was over $89,000, much higher than the median search cost of less than $40,000 for owner/operator sites. Waste management sites had a significantly higher median search cost of over $208,000. Sites with de minimis parties had an even higher median cost of about $253,000.

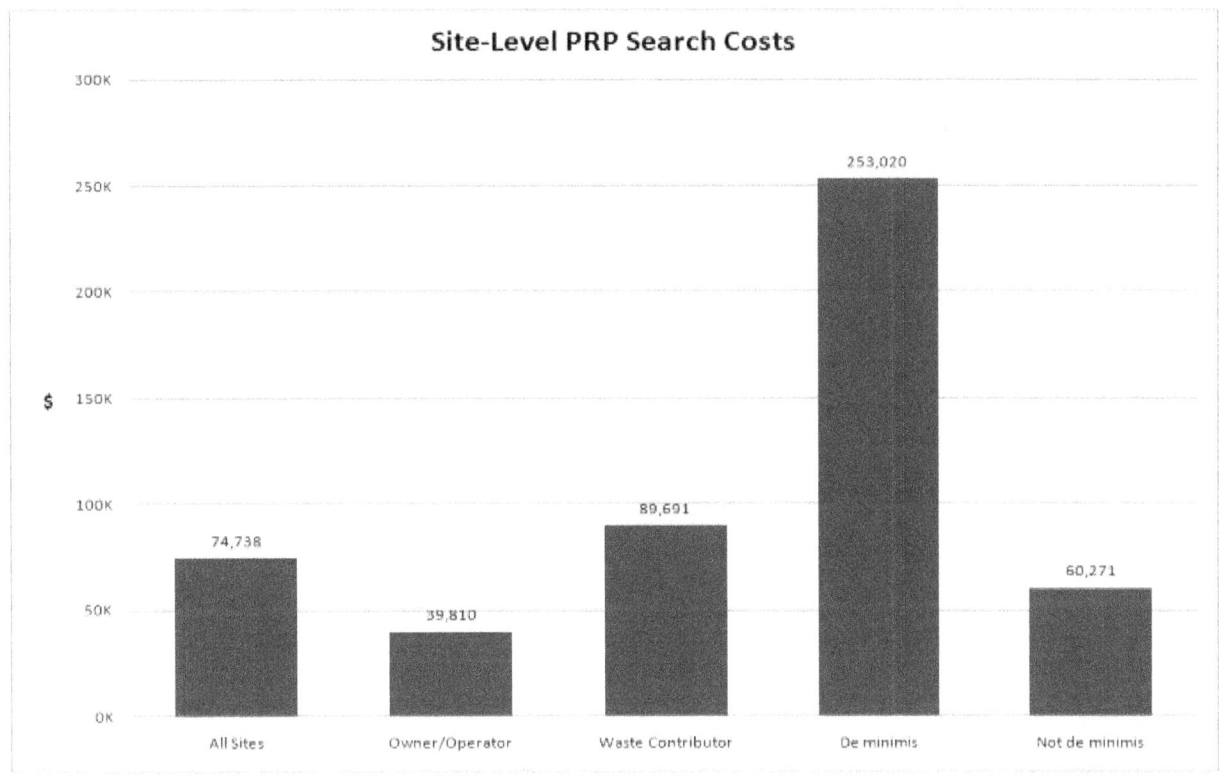

As the number of PRP determinations increased, so did total PRP search costs.

Determinations vs Search Costs
All Sites

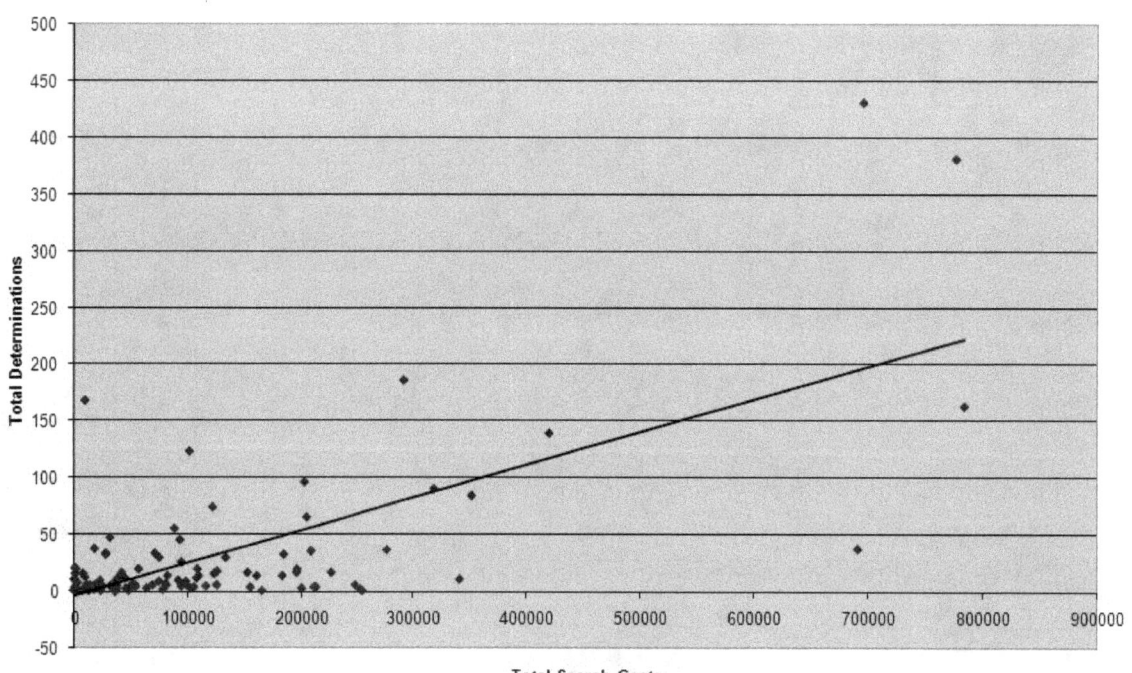

Regional Data Analysis of PRP Search Costs

Median PRP search costs were highly variable across regions, ranging from $20,000 to over $300,000 per site. The greatest variability was in owner/operator sites where the median ranged from a low of just under $3,000 in Region 5 to a high of $200,000 to $300,000 in Regions 8 and 9. The high medians in Regions 8 and 9 may be explained by the prevalence of mining and area-wide ground water contamination sites, which involve ownership of many parcels of property spread over hundreds of square miles. Breakdowns of the study universe by region and site type, however, generally produced regional universes that were too small to constitute statistically valid samples for analysis of variation in median search costs. (Region 1 had no owner/operator sites that satisfied the criteria for inclusion in the study universe.)

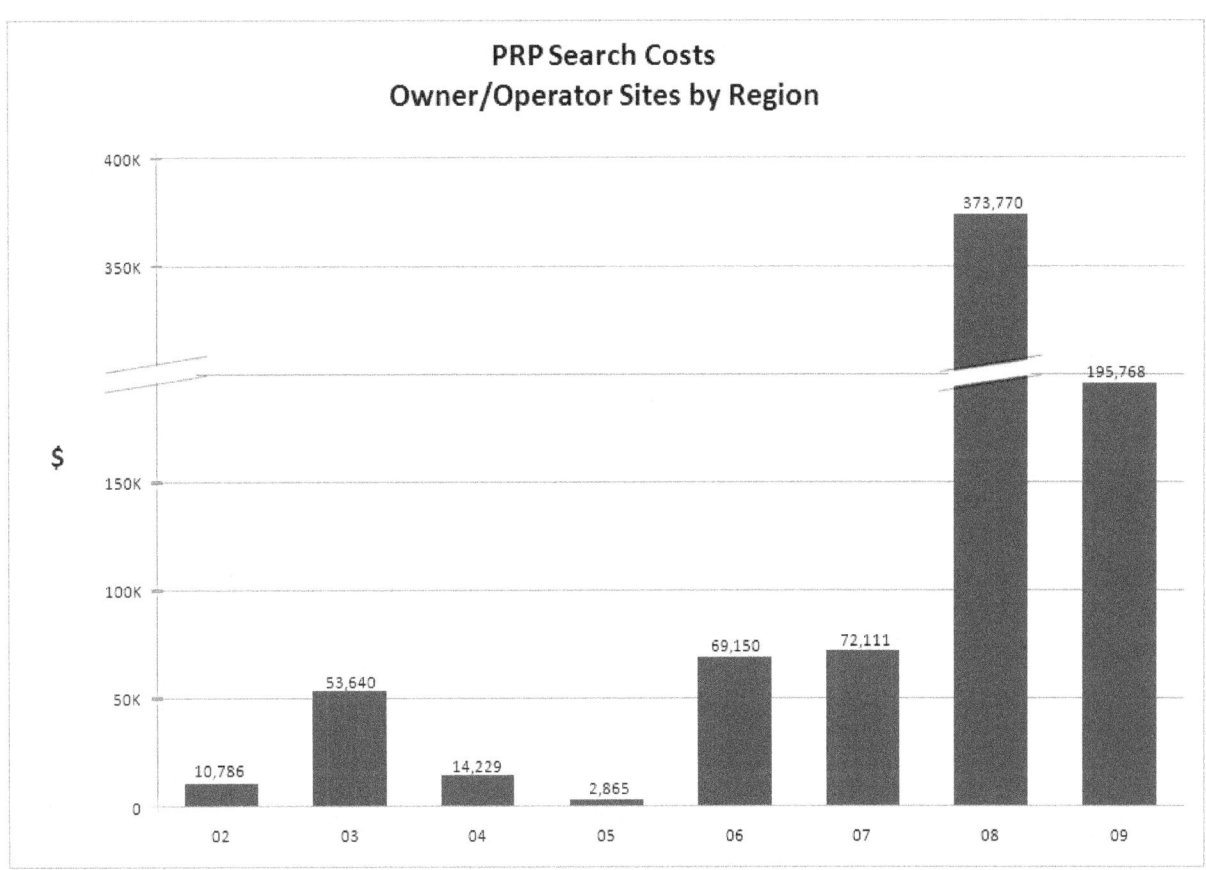

The median cost of PRP searches at waste contributor sites was more consistent, with costs ranging between $70,000 and $150,000. Regions 2, 4, and 5 generally had lower costs, and Region 9 had substantially higher median total search costs at waste contributor sites. Total search costs appear to be highly variable and very dependent on the nature and extent of the sites being addressed in the region, and may reflect prevailing wage levels and other cost of living factors beyond the scope of the study. In all regions, median total PRP search costs at owner/operator sites were lower than at waste contributor sites.

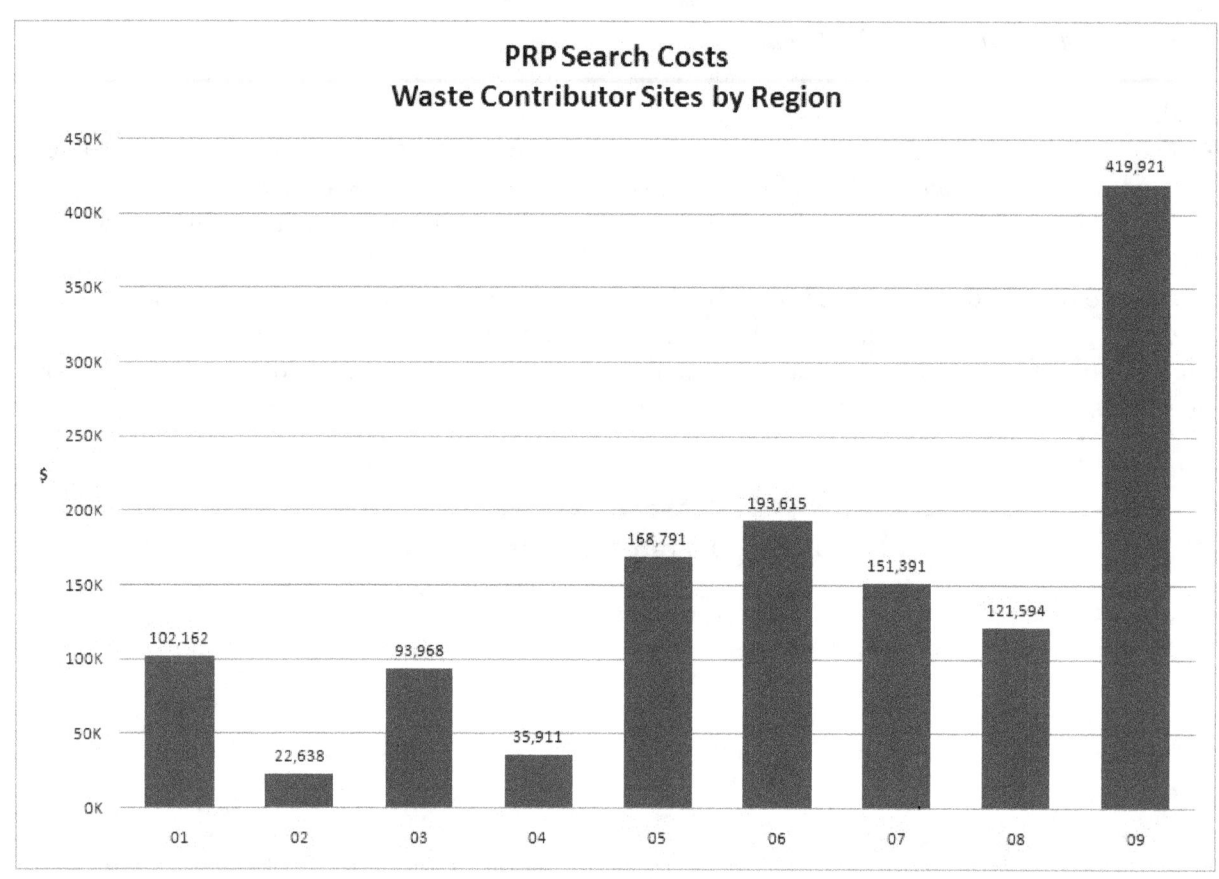

PRP Search Costs
Waste Contributor Sites by Region

2. Cost Per Determination (CPD)

CPD varied less than PRP search costs. The median value was $5,100 per determination. CPD was generally higher at owner/operator sites (slightly more than $8,600 per determination) than at waste contributor sites (nearly $4,300 per determination).

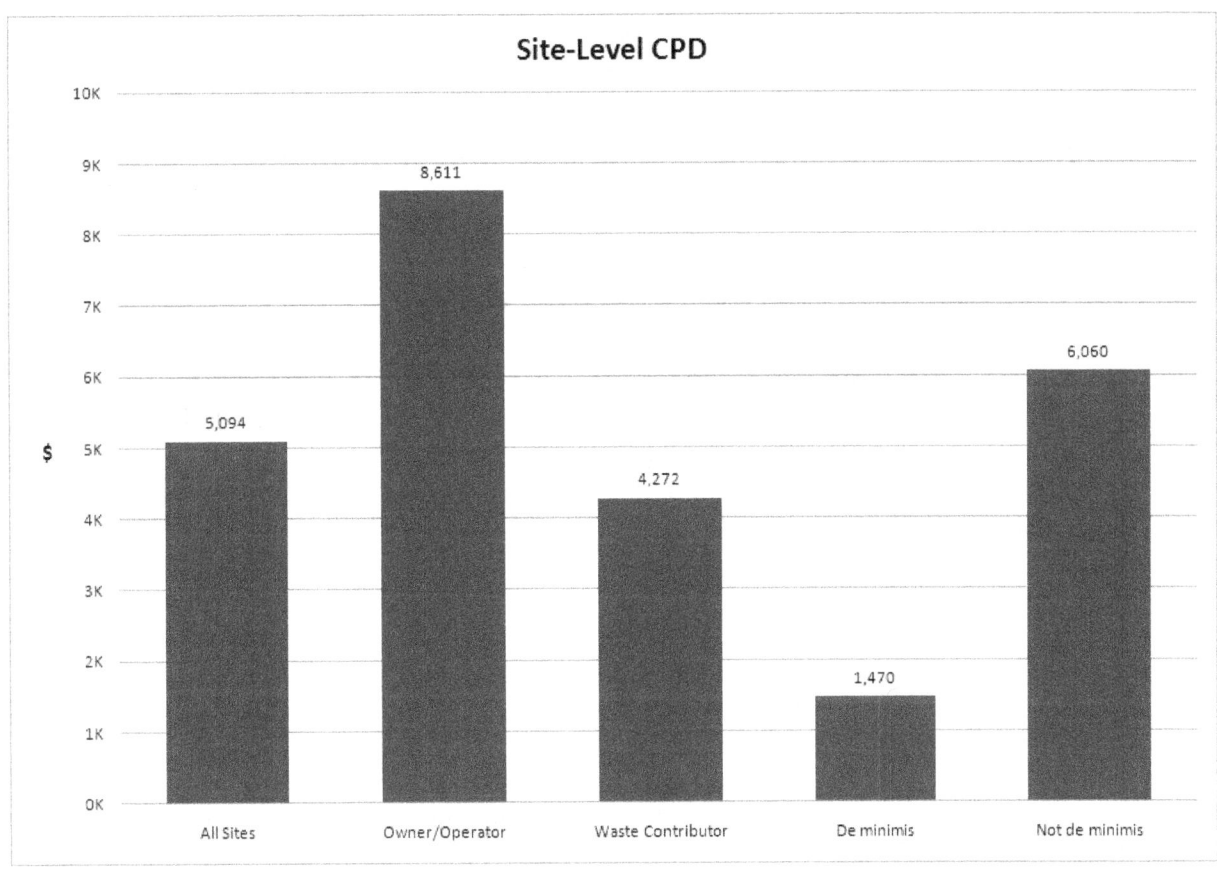

Sites with de minimis parties had the lowest CPD (just under $1,500 per determination) despite having the highest median search costs.

As the number of PRP determinations increased, the cost per PRP determination decreased.

Regional Data Analysis of CPD

Regional variability narrowed considerably when the CPD metric was used, although it did not disappear. Median CPD ranged from a low of about $1,500 in Region 5 to just over $13,000 in Region 6, but fell between about $2,000 and $5,000 in most regions.

Looking at owner/operator sites, median CPD in seven of the nine regions analyzed was in the $10,000 to $20,000 range. Determining the owners/operators at a site appears to be a "base" cost probably incurred in obtaining land title records and history and in conducting financial analyses of current and past owners/operators. These base costs would likely have to be incurred at waste contributor sites as well.

Median CPD was generally lower at waste contributor sites than at owner operator sites, ranging from $2,000 to $13,000 per determination. With the exception of Region 2, median CPD was lower at waste contributor sites than at owner/operator sites. This result is likely attributable to economies of scale; once the base cost is incurred, the cost of identifying each additional party declines as demonstrated in the preceding graph.

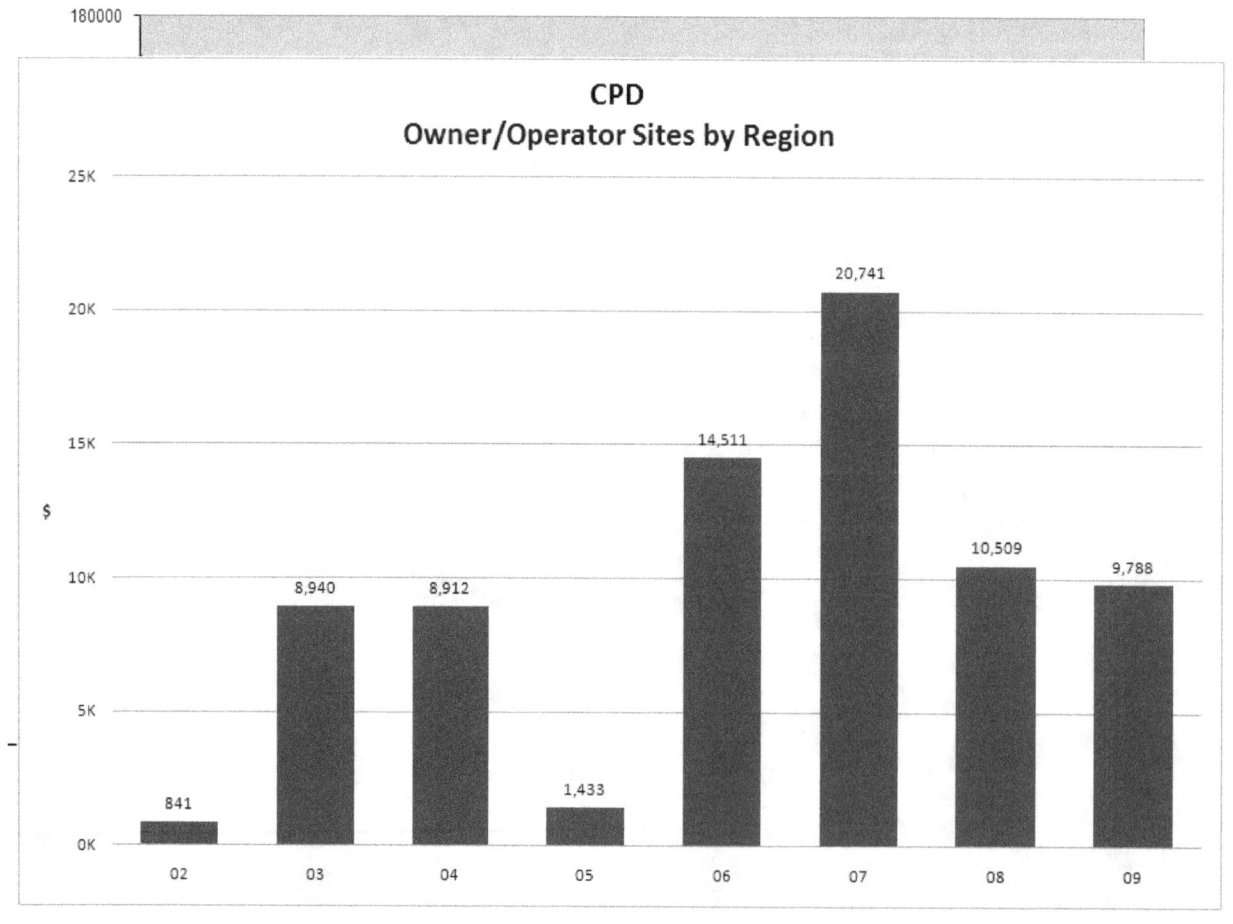

CPD vs. Number of Determinations
All Sites

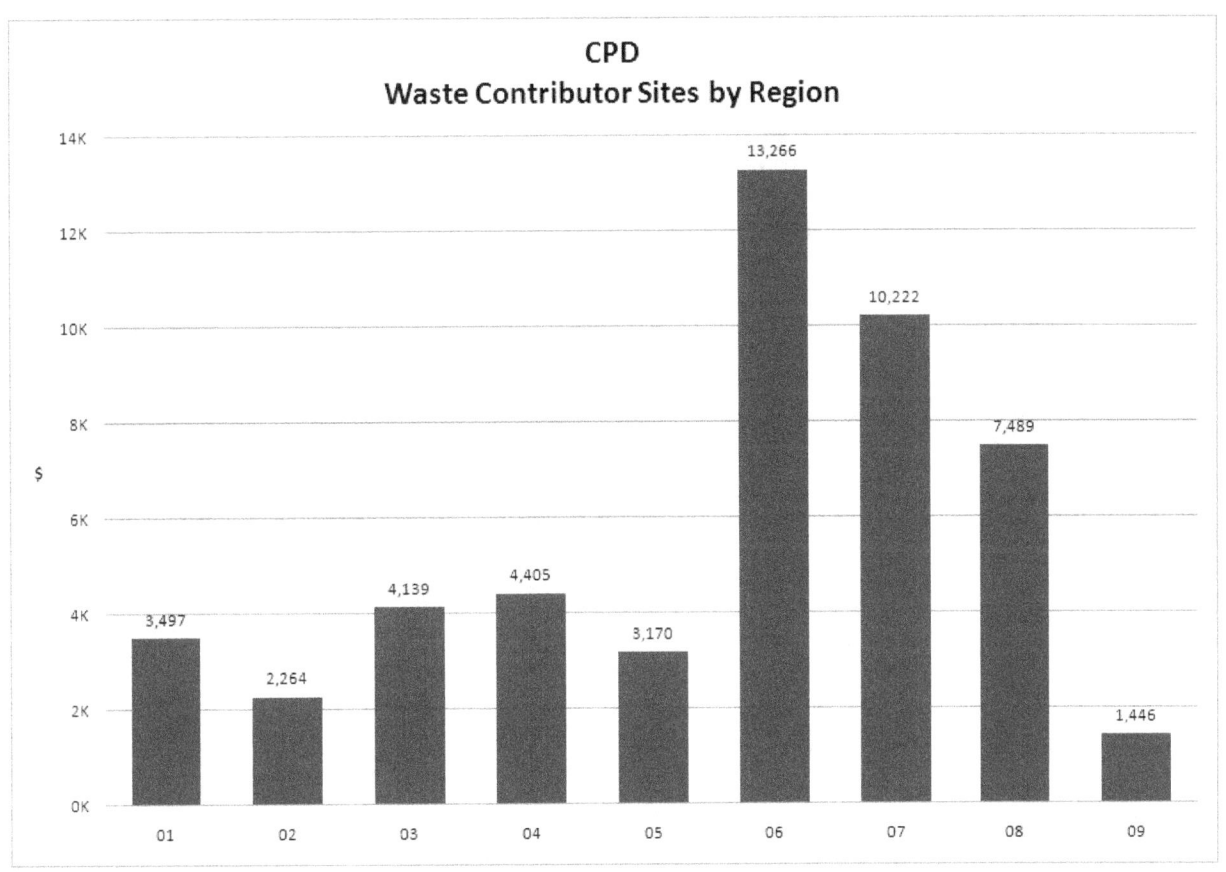

CPD
Waste Contributor Sites by Region

Further analysis of the regions at the extremes of the CPD continuum might reveal whether unique site attributes or PRP search practices were responsible for the high and low readings. Such insight might either suggest appropriate corrective action to control costs or highlight search practices that can be shared with other regions to improve efficiency.

3.   Return on Investment (ROI)

EPA spent over $30 million in direct and indirect costs on PRP searches at the sites in the study. As a result of those expenditures, EPA achieved PRP commitments of over $1.6 billion for future work and cost recovery. This represents a return on EPA's PRP search investment (ROI) of over 50-to-1. The ROI tended to be higher at owner/operator sites (65-to-1) than at waste contributor sites (40-to-1). Sites with de minimis parties had an ROI similar to that for the overall site universe. Regardless of variations among regions, all regions earn a substantial return on their PRP search investment, suggesting that further investment in this area would yield additional and comparable returns at all sites.

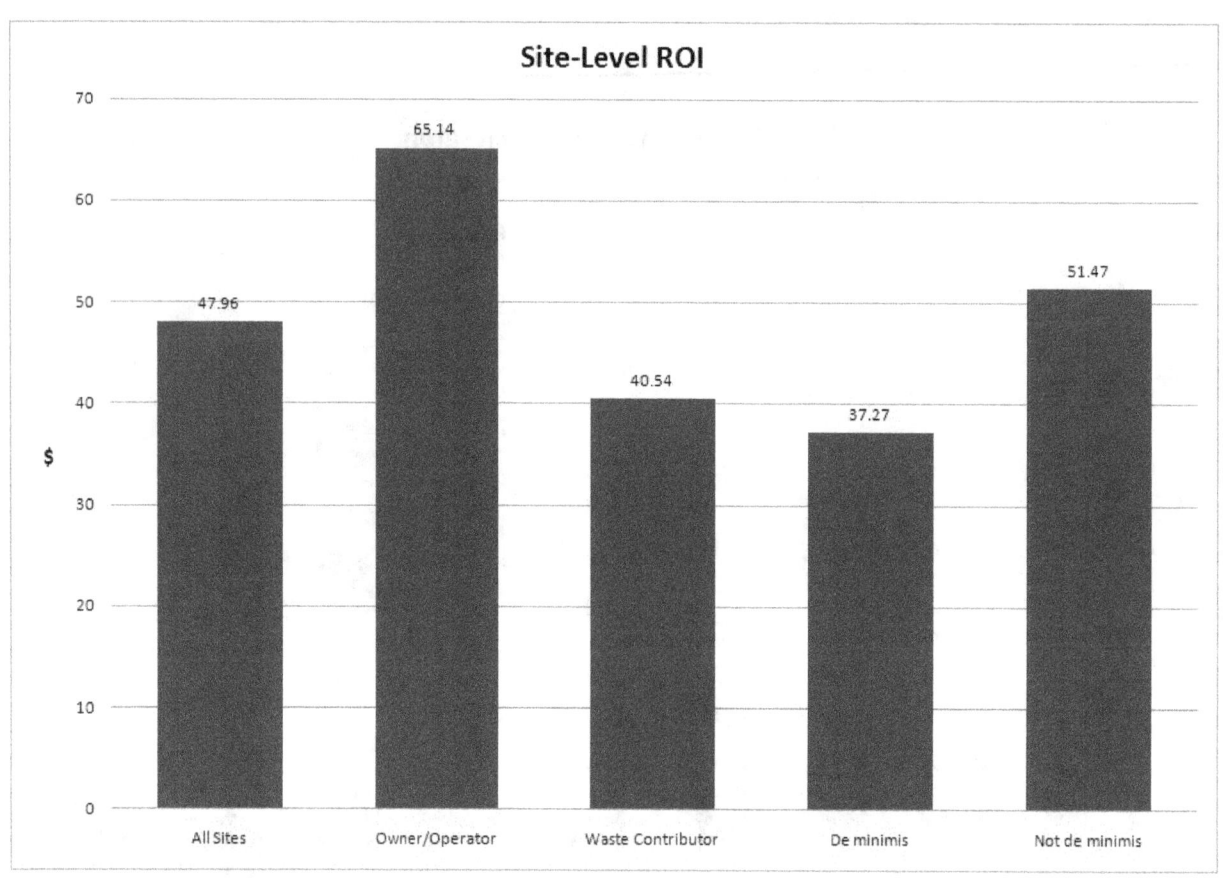

Site-Level ROI

Regional Data Analysis of ROI

With the exception of Region 6, median return on PRP search investment was very high, achieving between $40 and $250 in commitments for response and cost recovery for every dollar invested in PRP searches. Owner/operator site ROI varied considerably. ROI ranged between 40-to-1 and 300-to-1 in five regions. Two regions achieved owner/operator site ROI exceeding 10,000-to-1, while Region 6 had a low ROI of 4-to-1, an order of magnitude below the next lowest region.

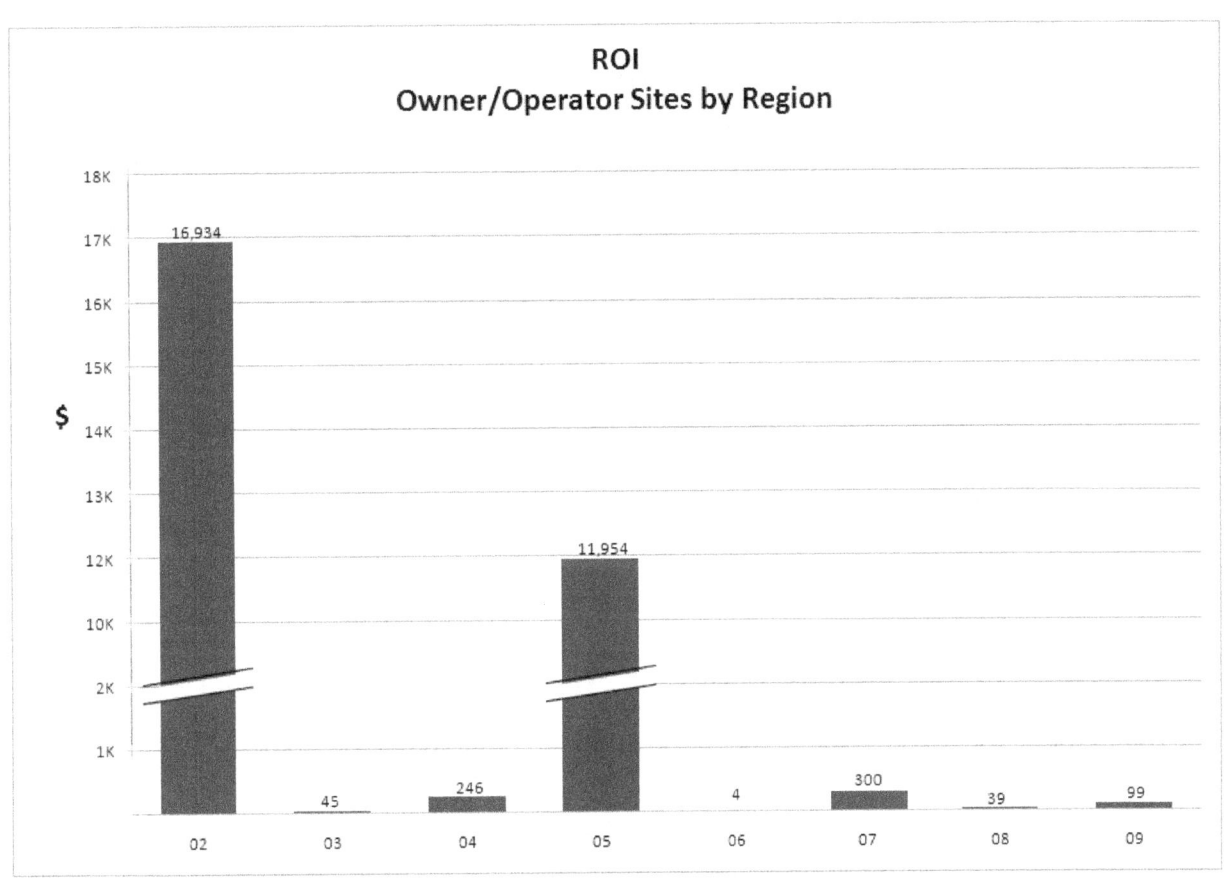

ROI
Owner/Operator Sites by Region

With the exception of Region 3, median ROI was generally lower at waste contributor sites than at owner/operator sites. This result may be attributable to the larger number of PRPs generally found at waste contributor sites. Region 3 had only one owner/operator site, a Fund-lead site where a comprehensive search was conducted with no positive identification of PRPs. This site's ROI constituted the de facto median and may not be typical of results to be expected at other owner/operator sites.

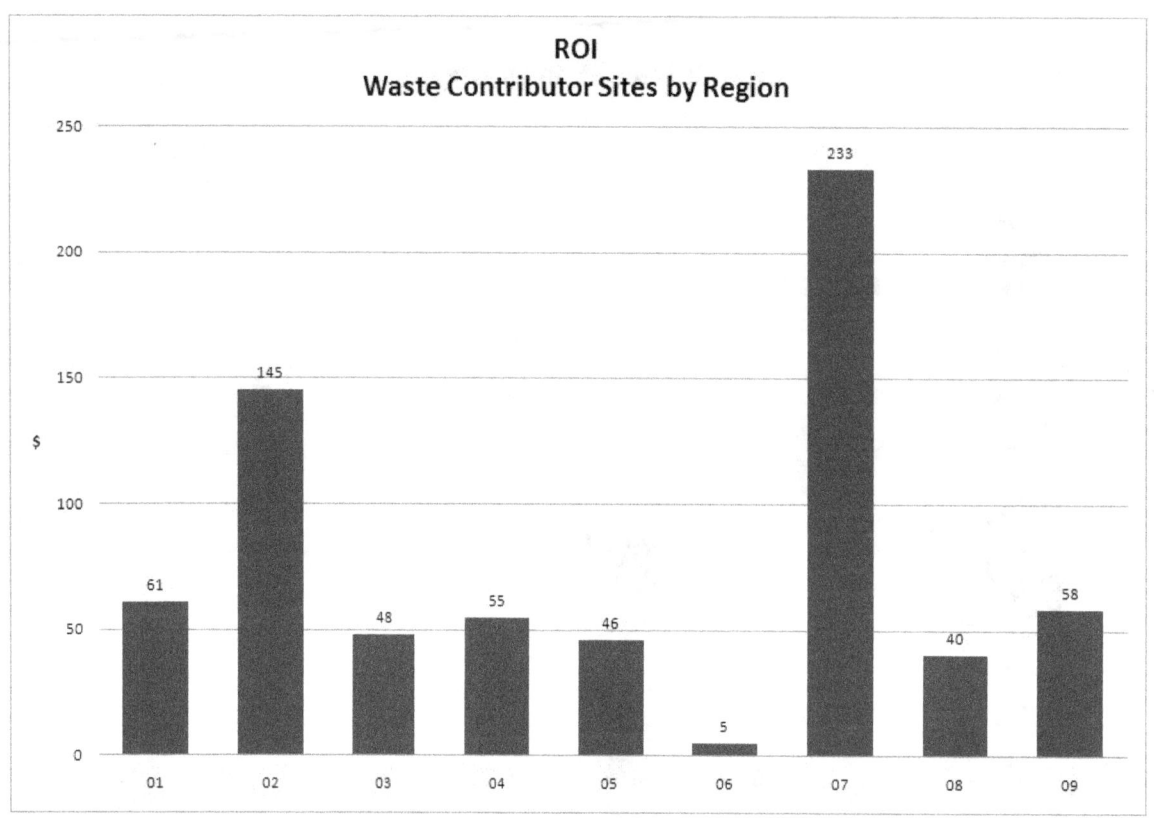

OSRE has had initial discussions with Region 6 on the lower ROI and will be conducting further evaluation to determine whether this is the result of data quality or is a programmatic issue that requires further in-depth evaluation. Further research may also be advisable in Region 7 in view of its extremely high ROI at waste contributor sites.

4.   Search Costs as a Percentage of Total Response Costs

PRP search costs were compared to the total of EPA expenditures plus any estimated future PRP work to be performed. The mean for all sites was just over 6% of total response costs. The mean was just over 1% of total response costs at owner/operator sites compared to nearly 8% at waste contributor sites. Waste management sites had the highest percentage at just over 19% of response costs. At one waste management site, search costs accounted for 70% of response costs. OSRE suspects that not all settlements at the site have been completed, resulting in under-reporting of total response costs.

B.   Characterization of Regional PRP Search Programs

In addition to collecting total response and PRP search data, EPA administered a questionnaire (Appendix B) to the regions asking for information on qualitative and quantitative characteristics of their PRP search programs to determine if those characteristics may have affected CPDs for their searches. While OSRE did not feel that the data were of sufficient consistency to compare to the site-specific results, responses to the programmatic questionnaire provide the following insights into regional PRP search programs.

1. Organization

Regions were evenly split between those that did and did not have separate organizational units that were predominantly concerned either with remedial or removal PRP searches or with both. The regions that did organize into such units – Regions 1, 3, 4, 5, and 9 – tended to be the larger ones. Regions 1 and 3 combined PRP search and cost recovery in the same branch or section. This practice is consistent with draft work elements issued by the Superfund Workload Assessment Project's Enforcement and Legal Support Subgroup, which included cost recovery activities in the Potentially Responsible Party (PRP) Search and Notification work element. Given the association of PRP search and cost recovery functions, Regions 1 and 3 were considered to have separate PRP search organizational units even though Regions 4, 5, and 9 assigned PRP search and cost recovery functions in different organizational units.

Staff members are spread more thinly in smaller regions, and this fact is reflected in the way those regions were organized. According to Region 7, for example, "(N)o one employee is dedicated to remedial PRP search tasks – not to remedial exclusively, nor removal exclusively. All aspects of PRP searches are spread among SF program, ORC, and Finance."

2. PRP Search Job Classifications

PRP search activities are conducted by staff members in a wide variety of job classifications, including attorneys, paralegals, civil investigators, enforcement specialists, cost recovery specialists, program specialists, remedial project managers (RPMs), and financial analysts, among others. Any of these job classifications may be dedicated to PRP search activities, depending on the requirements of particular searches and the availability of suitable staff members to perform them. The job classification most commonly dedicated to PRP search tasks, however, is civil investigator. All regions that dedicated any staff members to PRP search activities dedicated CIs, and two regions dedicated only CIs. The three regions that did not dedicate any job classifications to PRP search activities – Regions 7, 8, and 10 – were smaller regions whose size and resources precluded such specialization.

3. Site-Specific Case Teams

The practice of organizing site-specific case teams to conduct remedial PRP searches was widespread throughout the regions. As they were site-specific, teams varied as to the staff assigned to them and other functions they might be asked to perform. At a minimum, however, they most often consisted of the RPM, a regional attorney, and one other staff member, often a CI, compliance officer or other enforcement specialist. Participation in the team fluctuates as the PRP search progresses. Region 3, for example, reported that, "In addition, depending on the stage of the Site and the activity involved at various times, managers and specialists (toxicologists, hydrogeologists, etc.) will participate in team meetings."

4. PRP Search Support Contracts

Most regions also had a contract or work assignment to obtain support in performing PRP search-related tasks. These were usually enforcement support contracts under which a variety of services may be procured, including PRP search, litigation support, and community involvement support. One region obtained enforcement support services, including PRP search support, through work assignments issued under a REPA Zone contract. It was standard practice in all regions to appoint a staff member to oversee contractor performance of PRP search-related tasks, although the job classifications of the appointed staff members varied. Contractor oversight was performed by CIs in Regions 3 and 4, for example, while other regions appointed other classifications to perform oversight as work assignment managers.

5. Nature of Contractor Support

Contractors are used to perform a multitude of different tasks, but the tasks can be grouped into two major types. The first consisted of skilled research and technical tasks. The most common of these was title searches, which were performed by contractors in eight regions. The list also included property appraisals; interviews; corporate, financial, site, and operational research; database development; aerial photography; waste stream analysis; map development; and technical expert support. The second major type consisted of less skilled albeit important clerical and data management tasks. These included address verification; record retrieval and review; document organization; correspondence preparation and tracking; and compiling of summaries, lists, and rankings. Some skilled research and technical tasks may be site- or region-specific. For example, Region 9 uses contractors for aerial photography, map development, waste stream analysis, and technical expert support, reflecting the presence of several large and complex area-wide ground water sites in that region.

6. Distribution of Extramural Expenditures

Extramural PRP search-related outlays are charged site-specifically except for those that have tasks that are applicable to multiple sites, e.g., development of transactional database software. In most regions, these outlays are concentrated heavily – 60 percent to 94 percent – in the area of case development. Outlays for legal and financial analysis and documentation are less common, but still account for approximately 20 percent of outlays except in Region 10, where its response indicated that legal analysis/documentation accounts for 50 percent of extramural outlays. It is unclear why Region 10 is anomalous in this area, but it may be the result of a differing interpretation of the survey question or the fact that Region 10 has only one CI dedicated to PRP searches and utilizes extramural support in this area to supplement in-house expertise. These results are consistent with the tendency to use contractors to perform skilled research and technical tasks, and with the following comment from Region 10: "(W)e try to do as much as we can with limited in-house resources and sparingly use our extramural $ for very specific skills that cannot be handled internally."

7. Use of Full-Time Equivalents (FTEs)

A large majority of FTEs allocated to regions for remedial PRP search-related tasks are charged site-specifically, regardless of the tasks they perform. Whether the time is charged site-specifically or otherwise, remedial PRP search-related FTEs are used to perform predominantly case development and legal analysis/documentation tasks. Some part of a region's remedial PRP search-related FTEs may be charged by organizational units that are not dedicated exclusively to performing remedial PRP search-related tasks, however, even in regions where such dedicated organizational units exist.

Enforcement FTEs that are not specifically assigned to PRP search-related tasks are distributed among regions' functional units, e.g., ORC. Within these functional units, however, such FTEs may be used to perform PRP search-related tasks and be charged site-specifically. As Region 9 commented, "In general, attorneys and RPMs are dedicated to a specific site/project and will work on enforcement issues, such as PRP search-related tasks, when they arise on a site." Enforcement FTEs not specifically assigned to PRP search-related tasks appear to be allocated primarily to ORC, program offices, and support and administrative functions.

8.   Allocation of PRP Search Funds

Regions allocate funds available for site-specific remedial PRP search-related activities on the basis of site-specific factors. These include the risks to human health and the environment posed by the site, the anticipated complexity of the search, the nature of anticipated search tasks, the likelihood of a PRP lead, and the potential value of settlement. Site-specific factors are weighed in preference to applying "rules of thumb" such as the relation PRP search costs should bear to estimated response costs. Only Region 8 indicated that it applied such a rule of thumb, i.e., that PRP search costs should generally be ≤10 percent of estimated response costs. This rule is consistent with the data for waste contributor sites discussed in "Search Costs as a Percentage of Total Response Costs" above. We suspect that it is based on the prevalence of mining sites in Region 8 and the region's long experience with them.

9.   PRP Search Planning and Progress

Just as they allocate PRP search funds after evaluating site-specific factors, so regions generally develop site-specific plans for conducting the search. These plans are subject to headquarters guidance, e.g., the *PRP Search Manual*[6] and *Superfund Program Implementation Manual*.[7] Several regions have developed their own manuals, which provide PRP search personnel with model letters, reports, logs, agendas, checklists, and summaries; instructions for accessing and using regional databases; and SOPs for performing search tasks, managing contracts, retrieving documents, and controlling correspondence, among other things.

Once searches are under way, regions assess their progress on an ongoing basis. Progress reviews may focus on what one region calls "critical junctures" in the Superfund pipeline, e.g.,

---

[6] *PRP Search Manual.* EPA 330-K-09-001, OECA, Office of Site Remediation Enforcement, September 2009.

[7] *Superfund Program Implementation Manual Fiscal Year 2009/2010.* OSWER Directive 9200.3-14-1G-T, March 31, 2009.

proposal for NPL listing, issuance of special notice letters for RI/FS or RD/RA, and SOLs for cost recovery, but PRP search teams are engaged in a process of continuous feedback. Some regions identify points in the pipeline by which they try to complete searches. Region 3 seeks to have a Notice Recommendation Memorandum completed four months before issuance of the ROD. Region 9 tries to complete its searches "during the remedial investigation process." Milestones are flexible and may be site-specific. At area-wide ground water sites, for example, the remedial investigation is a crucial investigative step for enforcement as well as response action purposes as identification of contaminants of concern serves to identify past and current facilities that may be responsible for contamination of the site.

10.   Initiation of the PRP Search

Most regions report that they initiate remedial PRP search activity during the PA/SI. This is also the point at which most regions assign an attorney and a CI or other enforcement specialist to the site. Some regions initiate searches during the HRS QA, and at some sites searches may be initiated during the removal phase. Assignment of a CI or other enforcement specialist to the site marks the beginning of the PRP search, and it is common practice to assign a site attorney at the same time. Some regions do not assign an attorney until they are ready to begin preparing Section 104(e) letters or they have drafted the initial PRP search report, but in all cases the assignment is made well before the site is proposed for inclusion on the NPL. There is a consensus within the program that the search should be initiated at the earliest appropriate time before the site is proposed for the NPL. Accordingly, the best practice would appear to be to assign both the regional attorney and CI or other enforcement specialist at the outset of the search unless specific site conditions or resource constraints render doing so inadvisable.

V. CONCLUSIONS AND RECOMMENDATIONS

Responses to the programmatic survey indicated a high degree of consistency in the way regional programs organize and perform PRP search-related tasks. Where sharp divisions are noticeable, they appear to be associated with regional size, resources, and the variety of site types or lack thereof in the region. Larger regions find it both feasible and efficient to implement more specialized divisions of labor. This pattern is evident in reliance on separate organizational units for and dedication of specific job classifications to PRP search activities.

Results of the programmatic survey indicate that the following are virtually standard procedures and may be regarded as practices that positively affect the timeliness and thoroughness of PRP searches:

- Initiate the PRP search at the earliest appropriate time before the site is proposed for inclusion on the NPL, generally during the PA/SI if listing is likely.
- Organize site-specific case teams to conduct the PRP search and include different specialists in the team as requirements of the search change.
- Assign a regional attorney and CI or other enforcement specialist to the site from the outset of the search.
- Manage PRP searches with reference to flexible, site-specific milestones set with the help of continuous feedback.
- Assign a staff member to oversee contractor performance of PRP search-related tasks.
- Use extramural resources in a "barbell" fashion to perform 1) highly skilled and specialized tasks, and 2) relatively unskilled clerical and data management tasks.
- Charge FTEs allocated to remedial PRP search-related tasks site-specifically.
- Allocate PRP search funds on the basis of site-specific factors, including risks to human health and the environment, complexity of the search, nature of anticipated search tasks, likelihood of a PRP lead, and potential value of settlement.

While it is not a standard practice, development of regional PRP search manuals, procedures and guidance that take into consideration regional organizational differences appears to be a growing trend. These resources generally contain detailed and jurisdiction-specific information that provides a valuable supplement to the national *PRP Search Manual*. Regions that have not begun developing their own manuals and guidance may find it useful to review those available from regions that have to determine if some valuable practices could be applicable to their region without having to "reinvent the wheel." In addition, some of these approaches could be shared among regions through monthly calls of the National PRP Search Enhancement Team and at the biennial National Training Conference on PRP Search Enhancement.

APPENDIX A

Site Universe Data

PRP Benchmarking and Best Practices Evaluation
Appendix A: Site Universe Data

Region	Site Name	O/O or Waste Contributor	GW Site	WM Site	De Min	Number of Determs.	Total Search Costs	Total Site Costs	CPD	Total PRP Commitments	ROI	Note 1	Note 2
01		Waste Contributor		Y	Y	91	318,218	2,024,623	3,497	10,889,305	34		
		Waste Contributor				3	102,162	1,389,102	34,054	2,500,000	24		
		Waste Contributor		Y		0	919	3,303,547	919	0	0		
		Waste Contributor			Y	12	44,915	8,749,084	3,743	18,700,991	416		
		Waste Contributor				14	160,348	6,805,745	11,453	14,000,000	87		
		Waste Contributor		Y		30	74,931	3,339,724	2,498	7,300,000	97		
		Waste Contributor		Y		80	1,422,660	4,709,038	17,783	2,634,129	2	*	
		Waste Contributor		Y		4	9,337	522,208	2,334	5,336,000	572		
		Waste Contributor				432	695,442	5,527,051	1,610	7,070,414	10		
02		Waste Contributor	Y			1	2,431	4,554,989	2,431	0	0		
		Waste Contributor		Y		34	27,760	57,228,185	816	822,387	30		
		Waste Contributor		Y		2	0	3,758,818	0	70,551,915	0		
		Waste Contributor				6	37,547	83,146,198	6,258	0	0		
		Owner/Operator				33	27,760	38,079,596	841	27,052,305	975		
		Owner/Operator				11	58	1,864,932	5	3,989,332	68,339		

Note 1: Site is excluded from charts of determinations vs. search costs.
Note 2: Site is excluded from charts of CPD vs. determinations.

1

PRP Benchmarking and Best Practices Evaluation
Appendix A: Site Universe Data

Region	Site Name	O/O or Waste Contributor	GW Site	WM Site	De Min	Number of Determs.	Total Search Costs	Total Site Costs	CPD	Total PRP Commitments	ROI	Note 1	Note 2
		Owner/Operator	Y			2	99	17,827,072	49	3,250,000	32,893		
		Waste Contributor				10	22,638	12,148,738	2,264	0	0		
		Waste Contributor				97	202,354	5,193,041	2,086	9,539,092	47		
		Owner/Operator				6	18,487	85,453,300	3,081	0	0		
		Waste Contributor				16	913	3,623,505	57	6,353,471	6,961		
		Owner/Operator				1	0	5,265,455	0	21,894,439	0		
		Waste Contributor	Y			20	1,509	32,207,383	75	8,050,000	5,336		
		Waste Contributor		Y		7	36,131	6,784,449	5,162		0		
		Owner/Operator				6	10,786	384,148,964	1,798	526,079	49		
		Waste Contributor		Y		4	21,553	1,114,048	5,388	3,130,013	145		
03		Waste Contributor	Y	Y	Y	85	351,851	0	4,139	9,104,065	26		
		Waste Contributor				14	82,079	0	5,863	5,210,000	63		
		Waste Contributor				1	0	0	0	1,598,194	0		
		Waste Contributor				6	247,717	0	41,286	1,147,331	5		
		Waste Contributor		Y		36	208,098	0	5,780	0	0		
		Waste Contributor				6	19,478	0	3,246	53,611,360	2,752		

Note 1: Site is excluded from charts of determinations vs. search costs.
Note 2: Site is excluded from charts of CPD vs. determinations.

2

PRP Benchmarking and Best Practices Evaluation
Appendix A: Site Universe Data

Region	Site Name	O/O or Waste Contributor	GW Site	WM Site	De Min	Number of Determs.	Total Search Costs	Total Site Costs	CPD	Total PRP Commitments	ROI	Note 1	Note 2
		Waste Contributor	Y		Y	382	776,279	0	2,032	25,204,083	32		
		Waste Contributor			Y	26	94,198	0	3,623	44,997,865	478		
		Waste Contributor			Y	13	9,461	0	728	52,878,713	5,589		
		Waste Contributor				18	125,428	0	6,968	300,000	2		
		Owner/Operator				6	53,640	0	8,940	2,410,000	45		
		Waste Contributor				16	7,640	0	478	9,538,193	1,248		
		Waste Contributor				5	93,968	0	18,794	2,450,000	26		
		Waste Contributor		Y		46	92,857	0	2,019	42,530,089	458		
		Waste Contributor		Y		5	17,179	0	3,436	8,504,348	495		
		Waste Contributor			Y	1179	1,691,454	0	1,435	43,043,611	25	*	*
		Waste Contributor				10	91,291	0	9,129	7,400,000	81		
		Waste Contributor	Y			6	80,982	0	13,497	1,000	0		
		Waste Contributor		Y	Y	16	122,830	0	7,677	2,356,480	19		
		Waste Contributor				4	12,517	738,281	3,129	95,000	8		
04		Owner/Operator				1	2,454	158,464	2,454	12,008,158	4,894		

Note 1: Site is excluded from charts of determinations vs. search costs.
Note 2: Site is excluded from charts of CPD vs. determinations.

3

PRP Benchmarking and Best Practices Evaluation
Appendix A: Site Universe Data

Region	Site Name	O/O or Waste Contributor	GW Site	WM Site	De Min	Number of Determs.	Total Search Costs	Total Site Costs	CPD	Total PRP Commitments	ROI	Note 1	Note 2
		Waste Contributor				2	77,948	12,495,122	38,974	281,631	4		
		Waste Contributor				1	7,050	433,002	7,050	12,255,280	1,738		
		Waste Contributor				7	51,718	39,387,771	7,388	226,821	4		
		Waste Contributor	Y			6	14,085	2,125,993	2,347	0	0		
		Waste Contributor				7	34,160	889,283	4,880	0	0		
		Waste Contributor				11	39	1,054,417	4	0	0		
		Waste Contributor		Y		169	9,771	399,803	58	18,322,321	1,875		
		Waste Contributor				0	35,911	5,719,017	35,911	1,455,735	41		
		Waste Contributor				2	8,811	294,438	4,405	1,200,000	136		
		Waste Contributor				17	152,180	604,153	8,952	2,307,830	15		
		Waste Contributor				6	69,010	2,709,999	11,502	2,414,694	35		
		Waste Contributor				124	101,234	404,158	816	6,938,012	69		
		Waste Contributor				5	25,017	17,297,464	5,003	14,607,663	584		
		Owner/Operator				3	15,951	972,739	5,317	3,030,111	190		
		Owner/Operator				1	12,507	111,336	12,507	3,782,181	302		

Note 1: Site is excluded from charts of determinations vs. search costs.
Note 2: Site is excluded from charts of CPD vs. determinations.

4

PRP Benchmarking and Best Practices Evaluation
Appendix A: Site Universe Data

Region	Site Name	O/O or Waste Contributor	GW Site	WM Site	De Min	Number of Determs.	Total Search Costs	Total Site Costs	CPD	Total PRP Commitments	ROI	Note 1	Note 2
		Waste Contributor	Y			1	47,904	6,644,200	47,904	0	0		
		Waste Contributor				34	70,963	722,818	2,087	1,530,449	22		
		Waste Contributor			Y	1048	2,447	16,387,730	2	61,233,687	25,028	*	*
		Waste Contributor	Y			12	38,285	5,533,226	3,190	0	0		
		Owner/Operator				4	104,788	566,365	26,197	1,155,400	11		
		Waste Contributor			Y	682	132,483	15,174,353	194	1,222,939	9	*	
		Waste Contributor				4	428	745,319	107	6,954,400	16,251		
		Waste Contributor				4	0	803,390	0	6,766,409	0		
		Waste Contributor				4	48,815	19,814,704	12,204	24,666,373	505		
05		Waste Contributor			Y	1875	2,087	38,962,354	1	236,256,190	113,220	*	*
		Waste Contributor	Y			0	0	60,038	0	0	0		
		Waste Contributor			Y	164	783,574	842,567	4,778	956,200	1		
		Waste Contributor				1994	0	21,522,978	132,616	0	0	*	*
		Waste Contributor				10	1,326,158	1,819,349	132,616	175,000	0	*	*
		Owner/Operator				2	2,865	739,386	1,433	34,250,000	11,954		

Note 1: Site is excluded from charts of determinations vs. search costs.
Note 2: Site is excluded from charts of CPD vs. determinations.

5

PRP Benchmarking and Best Practices Evaluation
Appendix A: Site Universe Data

Region	Site Name	O/O or Waste Contributor	GW Site	WM Site	De Min	Number of Determs.	Total Search Costs	Total Site Costs	CPD	Total PRP Commitments	ROI	Note 1	Note 2
		Waste Contributor				3	45,403	428,434	15,134	4,020,291	89		
		Waste Contributor			Y	187	292,179	2,792,337	1,562	1,015,580	3		
		Waste Contributor				1	207	1,108,430	207	52,392,000	252,974		
		Waste Contributor		Y		4	210,963	69,516	52,741	0	0		
06		Waste Contributor				1	1,316,239	6,141,287	1,316,239	0	0	*	*
		Owner/Operator				3	37,851	11,968,226	12,617	0	0		
		Owner/Operator				17	41,769	162,613	2,457	1,820,072	44		
		Waste Contributor	Y			2	3,214	15,561,586	1,607	0	0		
		Waste Contributor				2	17,424	13,044,959	8,712	0	0		
		Owner/Operator	Y			4	21,388	4,072,382	5,347	0	0		
		Owner/Operator	Y			3	199,867	4,486,312	66,622	800,000	4		
		Waste Contributor	Y			14	182,900	354,913	13,064	1,500,000	8		
		Owner/Operator				9	74,545	10,053,616	8,283	300,575	4		
		Owner/Operator	Y			3	15,077	14,548,644	5,026	0	0		
		Owner/Operator				6	98,436	7,365,358	16,406	0	0		
		Waste Contributor	Y		Y	2000	2,986,563	9,446,006	1,493	6,517,021	2	*	*
		Owner/Operator				5	31,609	4,357,731	6,322	0	0		
		Owner/Operator	Y			1	23,448	2,536,369	23,448	0	0		

Note 1: Site is excluded from charts of determinations vs. search costs.
Note 2: Site is excluded from charts of CPD vs. determinations.

6

PRP Benchmarking and Best Practices Evaluation
Appendix A: Site Universe Data

Region	Site Name	O/O or Waste Contributor	GW Site	WM Site	De Min	Number of Determs.	Total Search Costs	Total Site Costs	CPD	Total PRP Commitments	ROI	Note 1	Note 2
		Owner/Operator				1	254,442	5,929,901	254,442	700,000	3		*
		Waste Contributor	Y			4	53,872	9,455,388	13,468	0	0		
		Owner/Operator				1	164,851	36,900,057	164,851	0	0		
		Owner/Operator				4	212,572	7,881,824	53,143	0	0		
		Waste Contributor	Y			66	204,330	2,145,984	3,096	1,021,180	5		
		Waste Contributor				6	125,079	177,832	20,846	2,211,192	18		
		Owner/Operator				3	63,754	13,465,219	21,251	0	0		
		Owner/Operator				7	80,369	3,353,229	11,481	5,235,000	65		
		Waste Contributor				11	340,755	365,705	30,978	1,110,000	3		
07		Waste Contributor	Y			17	195,367	26,106,593	11,492	800,001	4		
		Waste Contributor				12	107,415	64,318,452	8,951	49,614,540	462		
		Owner/Operator				1	36,075	5,741,431	36,075	20,063,213	556		
		Owner/Operator				20	108,146	1,468,565	5,407	4,706,224	44		
		Owner/Operator	Y			21	608	2,078,082	29	1,114,435	1,832		
		Owner/Operator				2	252,635	6,340,557	126,318	873,500	3		
		Waste Contributor				14	109,119	21,792,749	7,794	749,789	7		
08		Waste Contributor			Y	48	31,492	81,657,365	656	118,657,974	3,768		
		Owner/Operator				20	56,788	2,809,514	2,839	0	0		

Note 1: Site is excluded from charts of determinations vs. search costs.
Note 2: Site is excluded from charts of CPD vs. determinations.

7

PRP Benchmarking and Best Practices Evaluation
Appendix A: Site Universe Data

Region	Site Name	O/O or Waste Contributor	GW Site	WM Site	De Min	Number of Determs.	Total Search Costs	Total Site Costs	CPD	Total PRP Commitments	ROI	Note 1	Note 2
	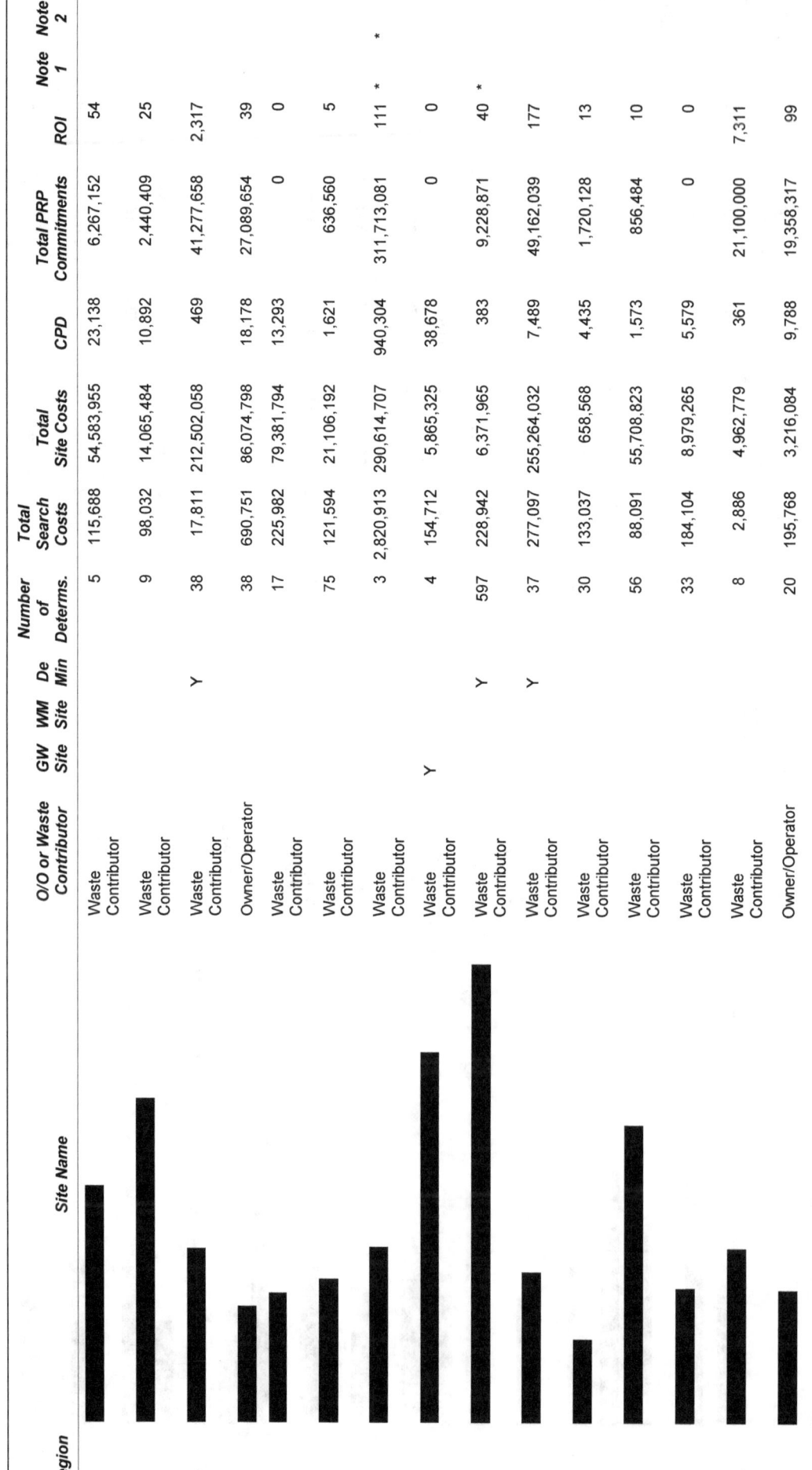	Waste Contributor				5	115,688	54,583,955	23,138	6,267,152	54		
		Waste Contributor				9	98,032	14,065,484	10,892	2,440,409	25		
		Waste Contributor			Y	38	17,811	212,502,058	469	41,277,658	2,317		
		Owner/Operator				38	690,751	86,074,798	18,178	27,089,654	39		
		Waste Contributor				17	225,982	79,381,794	13,293	0	0		
		Waste Contributor				75	121,594	21,106,192	1,621	636,560	5		
		Waste Contributor				3	2,820,913	290,614,707	940,304	311,713,081	111	*	*
		Waste Contributor	Y			4	154,712	5,865,325	38,678	0	0		
		Waste Contributor			Y	597	228,942	6,371,965	383	9,228,871	40	*	
		Waste Contributor			Y	37	277,097	255,264,032	7,489	49,162,039	177		
		Waste Contributor				30	133,037	658,568	4,435	1,720,128	13		
		Waste Contributor				56	88,091	55,708,823	1,573	856,484	10		
09		Waste Contributor				33	184,104	8,979,265	5,579	0	0		
		Waste Contributor				8	2,886	4,962,779	361	21,100,000	7,311		
		Owner/Operator				20	195,768	3,216,084	9,788	19,358,317	99		

Note 1: Site is excluded from charts of determinations vs. search costs.
Note 2: Site is excluded from charts of CPD vs. determinations.

8

PRP Benchmarking and Best Practices Evaluation
Appendix A: Site Universe Data

Region	Site Name	O/O or Waste Contributor	GW Site	WM Site	De Min	Number of Determs.	Total Search Costs	Total Site Costs	CPD	Total PRP Commitments	ROI	Note 1	Note 2
		Waste Contributor		Y	Y	2866	4,144,802	16,645,639	1,446	33,703,516	8	*	*
		Waste Contributor	Y		Y	1907	1,505,171	5,126,277	789	79,527,913	53	*	*
		Waste Contributor		Y		140	419,921	9,877,221	2,999	26,803,606	64		
10		Waste Contributor				1	0	42,439	0	14,521,057	0	*	*
		Waste Contributor				8	97	56,161,583	12	0	0	*	*
		Waste Contributor				4	0	15,059,321	0	6,508,500	0	*	*
		Owner/Operator				10	117	5,724,438	12	16,864,000	143,636	*	*
		Owner/Operator				52	0	238,645	0	16,041,526	0	*	*

Note 1: Site is excluded from charts of determinations vs. search costs.
Note 2: Site is excluded from charts of CPD vs. determinations.

9

APPENDIX B

Programmatic Questionnaire

PRP SEARCH PROGRAM EVALUATION
PROGRAMMATIC QUESTIONNAIRE
REGION __

Organization

1. Does your Region have a separate organizational unit dedicated to any of the following?:

All PRP Searches	Yes _____	No _____
Some PRP Searches	Yes _____	No _____
Removal PRP Searches*	Yes _____	No _____
Remedial PRP Searches*	Yes _____	No _____
NPL PRP Searches	Yes _____	No _____
Non-NPL PRP Searches	Yes _____	No _____
(Check all that apply)		

If you checked "Yes" for any of the alternatives, please briefly describe the separate organizational unit and provide an organizational chart identifying dedicated PRP search units.

_____
_____
_____
_____

   * **Bruce:** Region 5 recently established separate sections for removal and remedial PRP searches.

2. Does your Region dedicate any of the following staff to PRP search activities?

Attorneys	Yes____	No____
Civil Investigators	Yes____	No____
Remedial Project Managers	Yes____	No____
On-Scene Coordinators	Yes____	No____
Financial Analysts	Yes____	No____
Case Developers	Yes____	No____
Enforcement Specialists	Yes____	No____
Cost Recovery Specialists	Yes____	No____
Environmental Protection Specialists	Yes____	No____
Community Relations Coordinators	Yes____	No____
Contractors	Yes____	No____
Other (e.g., specialized support)	Yes____	No____

If you checked "Other", please describe the type of dedicated staff.

_____

_____

_____

3. Does your Region organize site-specific PRP Search Case Teams?

     Yes_____   No_____

If you answered "No", please describe how your Region organizes to perform PRP search-related tasks.

_____

_____

_____

4. Does your Region have a dedicated contract or work assignment for conducting PRP search-related tasks?

     Yes_____   No_____

If you answered "Yes", please describe the contract or work assignment.

_____

_____

_____

5. Does your Region use multi-site work assignments for PRP search-related activities?

     Yes_____   No_____

6. Does your Region appoint a PRP Search Manager to oversee contractor performance of PRP search-related tasks?

     Yes_____   No_____

If you answered "No", please describe how your Region oversees contractor performance of PRP search-related tasks?

_____

_____

_____

7. Please describe the kinds of PRP search-related tasks your Region uses contractors to perform.

_____

_____

_____

8. Do any of the following factors affect the way a PRP search is organized or overseen in your Region?

Estimated overall site response costs	Yes_____	No_____
Type of site (e.g., area-wide groundwater)	Yes_____	No_____
Length of time a site was in use	Yes_____	No_____
Length of time has been abandoned	Yes_____	No_____
Community involvement	Yes_____	No_____
PRP involvement	Yes_____	No_____
Use of contractors	Yes_____	No_____
Removal activity	Yes_____	No_____
Other (e.g., no-site-specific factors)	Yes_____	No_____

If you checked "Yes" for any of the alternatives, please describe how the factor affects the organization or oversight of a PRP search.

_____

_____

_____

_____

Resources

9. Of the _____ FTE allocated to the Region for PRP search-related tasks, please indicate the number in each of the functional categories below and the number of FTE in each of those categories that charged greater than 5% of their time site-specifically.

	Number	Site-Specific
Case Development	_____	_____
Case Management	_____	_____
Investigation	_____	_____
Legal Analysis/Documentation	_____	_____
Financial Analysis/Documentation	_____	_____
Contract Management	_____	_____
Records Management	_____	_____
Administrative	_____	_____
Other	_____	_____

10. Of the _____ FTE allocated to the Region for PRP search-related tasks that are not identified in Question 6, please briefly describe the remaining FTE and where they are located within the regional organization. If possible, please provide an organizational chart that reflects your response.

_____

_____

_____

11. Extramural outlays on PRP search-related tasks in your Region from FY2000 through FY2005 were $_____. **[Data to be pre-populated from IFMS and verified by the Region.]**

How much of those outlays were site-specific? $_____

12. Of the total outlays in extramural PRP search-related tasks identified in Question 11, approximately how much was for tasks performed in each of the functional areas below?

	Percentage
Case Development	_____
Case Management	_____
Investigation	_____
Legal Analysis/Documentation	_____
Financial Analysis/Documentation	_____
Contract Management	_____
Records Management	_____
Administrative	_____
Other	_____

13. How does your Region determine what part of the funds available for PRP search-related activities to allocate to a particular site?

_____

_____

_____

14. Does your Region use any guidelines or rules of thumb as to the percentage of overall estimated site response costs that should be devoted to a PRP search?

Yes_____   No_____

If you answered "Yes", please describe the guidelines or rules of thumb.

_____
_____
_____

Policies and Procedures

15. Does your Region have written policies or procedures concerning PRP search-related activities?

> Yes_____   No_____

If you answered "Yes", please provide a copy of any and all applicable regional policies and procedures.

16. What factors do you weigh when assessing the prospects of identifying liable and viable PRPs at a site?

_____
_____
_____

17. SPIM states that a PRP search "should be initiated as soon as possible after the Region decides that a response . . . action is likely to be required at the site." What factors determine how long it takes your Region to initiate a PRP search once it decides that a response action is likely to be required?

Estimated overall site response costs	Yes____	No____
Type of site (e.g., area-wide groundwater)	Yes____	No____
Length of time a site was in use	Yes____	No____
Length of time has been abandoned	Yes____	No____
Community involvement	Yes____	No____
PRP involvement in search	Yes____	No____
Use of contractors	Yes____	No____
Site access issues	Yes____	No____
Resource constraints	Yes____	No____
Removal activity	Yes____	No____
Other (e.g., no-site-specific factors)	Yes____	No____

If you checked any factors "Yes", please explain how they affect initiation of the search.

_____
_____
_____

18. Do Case Teams in your Region develop site-specific PRP search plans?

      Yes_____   No_____

19. Does your Region generally conduct PRP searches in distinct phases?

      Yes_____   No_____

If you answered "Yes", please describe or characterize the phases.

_____

_____

_____

20. Please describe any milestones or rules of thumb used in your Region to assess the progress of a PRP search.

_____

_____

_____

21. Do staff performing PRP search-related tasks in your Region have open procurement authority?

      Yes_____   No_____

22. Does your Region use an early on-site responder's checklist?

      Yes_____   No_____

23. Does your Region use third-party neutrals to perform alternate dispute resolution ("ADR") functions in connection with PRP searches?

If you answered "Yes", please describe or characterize the functions that third-party neutrals have been asked to perform.

_____

_____

_____

APPENDIX C

Programmatic Questionnaire Responses

Organization	Region 1	Region 2	Region 3	Region 4	Region 5	Region 6	Region 7	Region 8	Region 9	Region 10
1. Does your Region have a separate organizational unit dedicated to any of the following?										
All PRP Searches	Yes	No	No	Yes	Blank	No	No	No	Blank	No
Removal PRP Searches	Yes	Blank	No	Blank	Yes	No	No	No	No	No
Remedial PRP Searches	Yes	No	No	Blank	Yes	No	No	No	Yes	No
If you checked "Yes" for any of the alternatives, please briefly describe the separate organizational unit and provide an organizational chart identifying dedicated PRP search units.	Technical & Enforcement Support Section		"Up until June 2005, Region 3 had a dedicated PRP Investigation Section with 4 Civil Investigators (CIs) who handled all Remedial Sites and a few large removals; a dedicated Removal Civil Investigator who was part of the Removal Branch and handled all Removal Sites requiring assistance; and a dedicated Cost Recovery Section with 1 CI, several Compliance Officers (COs) and 1 Cost Recovery Expert, all of whom did some PRP search work as part of Cost Recovery actions and occasionally assisted with removals. As part of the 2005 HSCD reorganization, the PRP Investigation Section, Cost Recovery Section and Removal CI were combined into the Cost Recovery Branch. An old organizational chart and a current organizational chart are attached."	"Specific branch (SEIMB) is responsible for performing/ coordinating PRP searches."	Emergency Enforcement Services Section (Removal), Remedial Enforcement Services Section (Remedial)			"PRP searches are conducted by one civil investigator and five senior enforcement specialists in the Technical Enforcement Program CERCLA/RCRA unit. This Program unit resides in the Office of Enforcement, Compliance and Environmental Justice. PRP searches are also supported by contracts."	"The Case Development Subteam in the Remedial Branch is the organizational unit designated for remedial site PRP Searches."	"The Office of Environmental Cleanup (ECL) houses **both** the remedial and removal programs. The Office also includes a Program Management Unit, which among other job functions, includes 0.5 FTE dedicated to PRP Searches (both remedial and removal) and 0.5 FTE dedicated to Cost Recovery."
2. Does your Region dedicate any of the following staff to remedial PRP search activities?										
Attorneys	Yes	No	Yes	Blank	Blank	Yes	No	No	No	No
Civil Investigators	Yes	Yes	Yes	Yes	Yes	Yes	No	No	Yes	No
Remedial Project Managers	Yes	No	No	Blank	Blank	Yes	No	No	No	No
Financial Analysts	Yes	No	Yes	Blank	Yes	No	No	No	Yes	No
Enforcement Specialists	Yes	No	No	Blank	Yes	Yes	No	No	Yes	No
Cost Recovery Specialists	Yes	No	No	Blank	Blank	Yes	No	No	Blank	No
Environmental Protection Specialists	Yes	No	Yes	Blank	Blank	Yes	No	No	Blank	No
Other (e.g., specialized support)	Yes	Blank	Yes	Blank	Yes	Yes	No	No	Yes	No

Organization	Region 1	Region 2	Region 3	Region 4	Region 5	Region 6	Region 7	Region 8	Region 9	Region 10
If you checked "Other", please describe the type of dedicated staff.	Paralegals		"Region 3 currently has 6 Civil Investigators in the Cost Recovery Branch who participate in PRP Search activities to varying degrees. Four of those investigators came from the now defunct PRP Investigation Section where they devoted their time, primarily, to remedial PRP searches. One investigator came from the former Removal Enforcement section where he conducted removal PRP searches. One investigator came from Cost Recovery where he conducted PRP searches as part of cost recovery actions and consulted on other matters. Five of the 6 CIs now have overlapping functions to some degree, the 6th continues to conduct only removal PRP searches. Four of the 6 CIs are also financial analysts. In addition, Region 3 has 1 cost recovery expert (job series EPS) who performs some PRP search work, and 4 Compliance Officers (COs) who perform some PRP search work. Two of the COs are Environmental Engineers, 1 is an EPS, and 1 is an Environmental Scientist. The bulk of the PRP search activities are conducted by CIs."	"CI are dedicated to all CERCLA PRP searches."	Program Specialist	"NPL Remedial Enforcement First Coordinator"		"All of the categories of staff listed above may work on a remedial PRP search but none are 'dedicated'. They also work on all other aspects of response and cost recovery enforcement functions for both removal and remedial."	"In general, attorneys and RPMs are dedicated to a specific site/project and will work with enforcement issues such as PRP search related tasks when they arise on a site. Region 9 defines the term 'PRP Searches' broadly in this document to include all related subsequent prep search enforcement activities. Region 9 defines 'dedicated' as constituting the majority of an employee's duties."	"Portions of FTE for these staff are used intermittently for PRP Search - no one position is *dedicated* to PRP search activities."
3. Does your Region organize site-specific remedial PRP Search Case Teams?	Yes		Yes	Yes	Yes	No	Yes	Yes	Yes	Yes
If you answered "No", please describe how your Region organizes to perform remedial PRP search-related tasks.			"Region 3 has remedial Site teams composed, generally, of a CI and/or CO, RPM, and attorney. The CI does the actual PRP search with technical input from the RPM and legal and other input from ORC. In addition, depending on the stage of the Site and the activity involved at various times, managers and specialists (tox, hydro, geo etc) will participate in team meetings. Region 3 is not sure if this is what you consider a site specific remedial PRP Search Case Team."			"Site teams, consisting of at least an RPM, an Enforcement Office and an Attorney are assigned to each site and this team is responsible for all activities at the assigned site, including PRP searches."				
4. Does your Region have a dedicated contract or work assignment for conducting PRP search-related tasks?	Yes		No	Yes	Yes	No	Yes	Yes	Yes	Yes

Organization	Region 1	Region 2	Region 3	Region 4	Region 5	Region 6	Region 7	Region 8	Region 9	Region 10
If you answered "Yes", please describe the contract or work assignment.	Title Search, Corporate Research, Interviewing		"Region 3 has an enforcement support contract with Chenaga Integrated Systems, LLC. That contract is approximately 50% Community Involvement, 50% PRP Search Support. Chenaga is contracted to perform most PRP search functions, including information gathering, address and corporate research, correspondence tracking, evidence summaries, waste-in lists, preliminary financial analysis, interviews, title searches, preparation of notice and Information request letters etc. The contract also includes takes for service of process, lien filings, FOIA support, negotiation support, litigation support etc."	"We have a contract in place (ESS) to address PRP search related tasks."	"It's an Enforcement Support Services (ESS) contract in which a number of work orders for specific activities are completed in support of Enforcement and Litigation activities for all types of Superfund and related sites."		"Enforcement Support Contract. Award date: 12/28/04. Contractor: Chenaga. Type: fixed price; Maximum contract value: $514,592.00; Project Officer: Jolleen Werst; Contract Officer: John Phillips. The PRP search work falls under Task Order 2."	"Enforcement Support Services 'ESS 3' contract (small business)."	"Region 9 has two enforcement support contracts with Science Applications International Corporation for PRP search related tasks and Arctic Slope Regional Corporation for indexing, copying and storage."	"In Region 10 we issue work assignments on a REPA Zone contract to procure enforcement support services from Booz Allen Hamilton."
5. Please describe the kinds of remedial PRP search-related tasks your Region uses contractors to perform.	"Same as above"		"Typically, Chenaga is used for general PRP search related tasks such as title searches, address verification, some corporate research, preparation of notice and information request letters, interviews and evidence summaries."	"Title search, address research, corporate research, record review/retrieval, interview witnesses (scripted), volumetric rankings, document organization."	"Title searches, property appraisals, preparing transactional databases, document reviews, waste-in-list preparation, address updates, mail and track enforcement letters."	"See Attachment"	"Title Searches, historical operations research; legal and factual search for information to support successor/parent liability arguments, case specific tasks as needed that do not fall into any specific category."	"All of the basic and specialized tasks identified in the EPA PRP Search Manual."	"1. Title Searches; 2. Corporate & Individual Research; 3 Letter Support (includes the creation of and may include correspondence tracking of 104e and Notice letters); 4. Interviews & Agency Data Collection; 5. Aerial Photography Collection and Review; 6. Map Creation; 7. Indexing, Copying and Review; 6. Map Creation; 7. Indexing, Copying and Storage; 8. Waste Stream Analyses; 9. Database Management; 10. Technical Expert Support."	"Review files and collect records, Organize records and track correspondence, Support drafting and issuing of information request letters, Perform title searches, Conduct business status and financial research, Develop site summary, Compile waste-in information, Classify PRPs, Prepare baseline PRP search report."
6. Does your Region appoint a PRP Search Manager to oversee contractor performance of remedial PRP search-related tasks?	No		No	No	Yes	Yes	Yes	Yes	Yes	Yes
If you answered "No", please describe how your Region oversees contractor performance of remedial PRP search-related tasks.	Work Assignment Manager		"All of Region 3's CIs are also certified Contracting Officer's Representatives. Each CI is responsible for acting as the Work Assignment Manager/COR for his or her specific Sites requiring contract support."	"Civil investigators serve as work assignment managers on PRP searches."						"Region 10 has an Enforcement Coordinator (1 FTE) who oversees contract support for PRP Searches (both remedial and removal) as well as Cost Recovery."
Resources										

	Region 1	Region 2	Region 3	Region 4	Region 5	Region 6	Region 7	Region 8	Region 9	Region 10
Organization										
7. Of the FTE allocated to the Region for remedial PRP search-related tasks, please indicate the number in each of the functional categories below and the number of FTE in each of those categories that charged greater than 5% of their time site-specifically.	"Unable to answer, at this time. Do not have information."						"We do not have the information to answer this question; to do so would require analysis of information that we do not keep. These activities are not separately accounted for in any SF timekeeping system nor are they accounted for by categorizing as remedial v. removal, nor specific to PRP search activities. If you want this kind of information, our timekeeping system needs to be much more exact."	"We are unable to answer this question. There are no FTE allocated solely to PRP search-related tasks. We have no basis for estimating these functional categories. We have no ability to pull this information from PeoplePlus."	"Please make a note, the FTE indicated [below] represents the FTE contributed by the Case Development Subteam only and does not include FTE from the Cost Recovery Subteam."	
Case Development			4.81/4.81	6/6	8.5/8.5	13/1			6/6	0.35
Legal Analysis/Documentation			1.924/1.924	6/6	5/5	10.00			Blank	0.3
Financial Analysis/Documentation			1.924/1.924	Blank	0.5/0.5	0.50			1/1	0.25
Contract Management			.962/.962	6/6	0.5/0	1.00			Blank	0.1
Records Management			0	Blank	Blank	1.00			0.5/0.5	0.2
Administrative			0	Blank	0.5/0.5	2.00			Blank	Blank
Other			0	Blank	Blank	3.5/1			Blank	Blank
8. Of the Superfund enforcement FTE NOT allocated by the Region for remedial PRP search-related tasks, please briefly describe the remaining FTE and where they are located within the regional organization. If possible, please provide an organizational chart that reflects your response.	"Attorneys and RPMs are dedicated to specific sites/projects and will work on enforcement issues."		"At the current time, Region 3, HSCD has approx 94.67 FTE being utilized for "enforcement" allocated as follows: 2.2 – Front Office; 2.9 – Federal Facilities (RPMs, managers, and administrative support staff); 28.3 – Remedial (RPMs, managers, and administrative support staff); 21.8 – Removal (OSC's, managers, and administrative support staff); 13.9 – Technical and Administrative Support (contracts, technical specialists, managers, administrative support staff); 4.5 – Community Involvement (CIC's, managers, administrative support staff); 21.07 – Enforcement (PRP Search, Cost Recovery, Cost Documentation, OH, and EPCRA staff, including CIs, COs, Cost Recovery Specialists, Cost Recovery Expert, inspectors, managers, administrative support staff). (continues)"	"Sixteen (16) FTE serve as enforcement project managers, coordinate negotiations, litigation support, cost recovery, etc. 1–Administrative Assistant, 1–Records Manager, 2–Workload Tracking, 1–Data Management."	154 Superfund enforcement FTE not allocated by the Region for remedial PRP search-related tasks. (continues)	"Remaining FTEs carry out other Superfund activities and provide support."	"We have provided organization charts; as you will see, no one employee is dedicated to remedial PRP search tasks not to remedial exclusively, nor removal exclusively. All aspects of PRP searches are spread among SF program, ORC, and Finance. We are a small region; dedicating any number of employees to a specific task is not cost effective; we need to have many talents in order to operate effectively. (continues)	"R8 receives 56.3 Superfund Enforcement (technical and legal) FTE. These FTE are distributed across the Region in every office."	"In general, attorneys and RPMs are dedicated to a specific site/project and will work on enforcement issues, such as PRP search related tasks, when they arise on a site. Therefore, the majority [of] the enforcement FTE are distributed to Office of Regional Counsel. The remaining enforcement FTE have been allocated to the following tasks/personnel/ units in Region 9: (continues)	"Region 10's Office of Environmental Cleanup (ECL) houses **both** the remedial and removal programs. There is also a Program Management Unit which among other job functions includes 0.5 FTE dedicated to PRP Searches (both remedial and removal) and 0.5 FTE dedicated to Cost Recovery. We also have portions of enforcement FTE in other offices, including Finance and ORC. A Civil Investigator (1 FTE) is located in the Office of Environmental Assessment (OEA) and supports removal PRP Searches as well as other regional programs."

	Organization	Region 1	Region 2	Region 3	Region 4	Region 5	Region 6	Region 7	Region 8	Region 9	Region 10
				"Of the 94.67 FTE, approximately 6.02 FTE are conducting remedial PRP search type work. A portion of those 6 FTE are located in the Office of Superfund Site Remediation (approx 1.76) and are distributed to RPMs, their managers, and administrative support staff. The remaining FTE (4.26) are located in the Cost Recovery Branch in the Office of Enforcement and are distributed to the CIs, COs, Cost Recovery Expert, our managers, and administrative support staff. Individuals in the Cost Recovery Branch conduct PRP searches to varying degrees, representing from nearly 100% of their time to none of their time. These individuals also have cost recovery responsibilities which are not counted in this survey. The Office of Regional Counsel also has 39 Superfund Enforcement FTE currently being utilized. Of those, approximately 3.6 FTE are conducting remedial PRP search type work. Region wide, there are approximately 9.62 FTE conducting remedial PRP search type work."		"The FTE are located in the Office of Regional Counsel, the Office of Public Affairs, the remedial response branches, emergency response branches, the Resources Management Division. These FTE are engaged in removal PRP searches, settlement negotiations, oversight of PRP lead response actions, preparation of cost documentation, and other enforcement actions.		That is reflected in our organization. We believe this an effective organization for us and that we benefit from cross-training between remedial and removal as well as the multitude of tasks that are encompassed within each program, including PRP search."		Removal PRP search (Superfund Division); Cost Recovery (Superfund Division); Superfund Program Support in Superfund Division (budget personnel, CERCLIS Mgmt. Specialist, Project Officer, Admin support), Other support groups in the Policy and Management Division (Cost Accounting, Contracts office)."	
9.	Of the total extramural outlays on remedial PRP search-related tasks in your Region from FY2003 through FY2005, what percentage of those outlays was site-specific?	100% All PRP search tasks are site-specific.		100%	100%	$1,877,422.00 / 100%	"Information not available."	"All PRP search tasks are site specific. (We're sort of curious how they could be non-site specific; perhaps using the information from one site to another where you have common PRPs.)"	100%	94%	"UNKNOWN. We cannot answer this question without seeing the outlay records that were the basis of HQ's total figure. However, HQ should be able to identify site-specific outlays by looking at the accounting for these records. In general, nearly all of out outlays should be site specific except for records management ($180K/year from enforcement funds) and a cost recovery SEE position ($40K/year). During this time period, one of our three contractor PRP search tasks was for a Fund lead removal site (Colville Post & Pole), and the outlays for it were $1,140."

5

Organization	Region 1	Region 2	Region 3	Region 4	Region 5	Region 6	Region 7	Region 8	Region 9	Region 10
10. Of the total extramural remedial PRP search-related outlays from FY2003 to FY2005, approximately how much was for tasks performed in each of the functional areas below?	"Unable to answer this question. To my knowledge, these activities are not separately accounted for"					"Information not available."	"We do not have the information to answer this question; to do so would require analysis of information that we do not keep. These activities are not separately accounted for in any SF timekeeping system nor are they accounted for by categorizing as remedial v. removal, nor specific to PRP search activities. If you want this kind of information, our timekeeping system needs to be much more exact."	"We are unable to answer this question. There are no action codes that correspond to these activities and no other valid way to determine costs."	"These are rough estimates."	
Case Development			70	60	88				94	25
Legal Analysis/Documentation			0	20	0				1	50
Financial Analysis/Documentation			20	5	3				0	10
Contract Management			0	3	0				5	Blank
Records Management			0	10	7					12
Administrative			10	2	0				0	3
Other			0	Blank	2				0	Blank
									"Separate extramural outlay."	
11. How does your Region determine the amount of funds available for remedial PRP search-related activities to allocate to a particular site?	"IGCEs are prepared based on the tasks to be performed, the amount of time estimated for each task, and the contractor's rates. Contractor dollars are continually tracked so available funds would be apparent."		"Independent Government Cost Estimates are prepared based on the tasks to be performed, the amount of time estimated for each task, and the contractor's rates. Generally, the CI (who is generally the work assignment manager for each Site needing contractor support) prepares the IGCE in consultation with the Site team and the Project Officer for the contract. Funds are allocated by yearly by the HSCD front office based on consultation with the work assignment manager and his or her manager based on projected work for the coming fiscal year."	"Contract dollars are continually tracked so available funds would be apparent."	"We assess complexity, difficulty, potential pay back, etc. and determine the most effective approach to conduct the search and allocate our resources: civil investigators, enforcement specialists, SEE's and contractors accordingly."	"Needs are evaluated on a site by site basis. Funds are made available based [on] the likelihood of a PRP lead and other factors."	"Extramural: the amount we get from HQ. Intramural: we believe we use our FTE to the maximum advantage to find PRPs. A complex PRP search case will get more intramural (and perhaps extramural resources) in order to get results; unfortunately, sometimes the result is that we have no PRPs or they are defunct, or in financial trouble. The difficult decision is when to feel comfortable that we have found everyone we can and to move on with fund financed cleanup. We again review PRP search information at cost recovery to determine if there is more information to support a finding of liability."	"PRP work assignment manager proposed a budget and seeks approval from management and the contracting officer."	"First, sites are prioritized within the Superfund Division based on the nature of contamination and risk at the site. From there, the case development team prioritizes the most critical sites where PRP searches are needed. Enforcement funding is then determined by the type of enforcement tasks thought to be needed to complete the PRP search. Prioritization of sites may change as new sites are discovered or various enforcement actions are necessary at a site (such as referrals and settlement negotiations). Ultimate prioritization is directed by the Branch Chief."	"As we in Region 10 watch our resources diminish, we try to do as much as we can with limited in-house resources and sparingly use our extramural $ for very specific skills that cannot be handled internally. We choose to use contract $ for mega sites due to their complexity and use of large data bases. The $ we get does not support the base program which is a vulnerability. For our SEE position, the incumbent has estimated he spends less than 5% of his time on PRP Search activities for remedial sites. There is a blanket amount given to OEA for travel and costs for the CI work on SF sites. OEA does not divide the $ among sites."
12. Does your Region use any guidelines or rules of thumb as to the percentage of overall estimated site response costs that should be devoted to a remedial PRP search?	No	No	No	No	No	No	No	Yes	No	No

Organization	Region 1	Region 2	Region 3	Region 4	Region 5	Region 6	Region 7	Region 8	Region 9	Region 10
If you answered "Yes", please describe the guidelines or rules of thumb								"Normally not to exceed 10% of response costs."	"Region 9 does not use any "rules of thumb" but instead reviews the progress of each site, along with the cost(s) of enforcement subtasks to be performed, in order to determine if the total cost of the enforcement subtasks are reasonable."	

Policies and Procedures

	Region 1	Region 2	Region 3	Region 4	Region 5	Region 6	Region 7	Region 8	Region 9	Region 10
13. Does your Region have written policies or procedures concerning remedial PRP search-related activities?	Yes		No	Yes	Yes	Yes	Yes	Yes	No	No
If you answered "Yes", please provide a copy of any and all applicable regional policies and procedures	"As mandated by HQ"			"Revised SOP in Draft form."	Blank	Blank	"They are attached."	"EPA PRP Search Manual"		"We refer to the National PRP Search Handbook."
14. Do Case Teams in your Region develop site-specific PRP search plans?	No		Yes	Yes	"Sometimes"	Yes	Yes	Yes	Yes	Yes
15. Please describe any milestones or rules of thumb used in your Region to assess the progress of a PRP search.	"Site enforcement teams meet on an ongoing basis and discuss status of PRP search activities."			"Each site has different requirements. Region 4 plans accordingly with input by attorneys, OSCS, RPM, EPMS."	"We conduct a title search, prepare and send 104(e) letters as needed, evaluate 104(e) responses, and conduct a civil investigation at each site. We evaluate the evidence and progress after each activity. Once these effects are complete, we assess the evidence and leads we have developed. We then decide what, if any, additional work is needed."	"Remedial PRP searches are tied to activities at the site, i.e., Proposal, SNL for RI/FS, SNL for RD/RA, Cost Recovery. Results of Searches are reported at these critical junctures with recommendations based on what is known at the time. A PRP Search is a continuing activity with several phases throughout the life of a site."	"We have case team meetings; an initial meeting is set up to determine the path to be taken, the resources needed and the time frame for completing those tasks to accommodate the needs of the site. Meetings follow as necessary, again, depending on the complexity and needs of the site."	"Site enforcement teams meet on a[n] on-going basis in order to discuss status of PRP search activities."	"The enforcement team reviews the progress of each site along with the associated enforcement costs on a continual basis. The site project team (i.e., attorney, RPM, case developer and at times a Section Chief) will review the progress of a PRP search to determine the next steps in the enforcement process. Region 9's enforcement objective is to have PRPs named during the remedial investigation process."	"We don't have any; it depends on the expectations of the RPM and case attorney and what they need immediately (e.g., owner/operator for access for removal action). After this the case team determines the appropriate steps/tasks necessary to complete a PRP Search for a site. In a nutshell, each one is tailored to site specific needs."
16. Does your Region have a system for prioritizing funding for remedial PRP searches?	No		No	Yes	No	Yes	No	Yes	Yes	No

Organization	Region 1	Region 2	Region 3	Region 4	Region 5	Region 6	Region 7	Region 8	Region 9	Region 10
If you answered "Yes", please describe your Region's system.				"Review needs according to available budget constraints."		"Remedial PRP searches are prioritized by the likelihood of finding PRPs, the phase the site is in and the potential contribution to the clean up of the site."		"Requests take into account projected new NPL site listings and on-going PRP search needs."	"The Region 9 enforcement team solicits enforcement needs from the RPMs and attorneys and reviews upcoming SOLs to determine priorities for funding PRP searches. The enforcement subteam meets with the Branch Chief to determine final prioritization for sites and funding for PRP searches."	
17. At what point in an NPL site's life-cycle does your Region initiate remedial PRP search activity?						"Remedial PRP Searches are initiated when the NPL Coordinator and the Remedial Enforcement First Coordinator agree that it is likely a site will be proposed to the NPL at some point in time. Usually this is between nine months and a year before actual proposal."				"It varies but usually during PA/SI Phase."
PA/SI Phase	X						X			X
HRS QA			X	X				X		
NPL Proposal									X	
NPL Final										
Post-RI/FS Start										
Post-RA Start										
Other					X					
If you answered "Other", please identify the point at which your Region initiates remedial PRP search activity.					"We initiate a remedial PRP search when a removal site transfers from the OSC to RPM. For an SA site we initiate the search when it comes from the state. Searches at other sites are initiated as soon as the remedial program becomes aware of the site."					

8

	Organization	Region 1	Region 2	Region 3	Region 4	Region 5	Region 6	Region 7	Region 8	Region 9	Region 10
18.	At what point in an NPL site's life-cycle does your Region assign an enforcement specialist/civil investigator to the site?						"An Enforcement Officer is assigned to a remedial site when the NPL Coordinator and the Remedial Enforcement First Coordinator agree that a site is likely to be proposed to the NPL."	"We do not have civil investigators or enforcement specialists; we do have paralegals who functionally perform the same tasks."			
	PA/SI Phase	X			X			X			X
	HRS QA			X					X		
	NPL Proposal									X	
	NPL Final										
	Post-RI/FS Start										
	Post-RA Start										
	Other					X				X	
	If you answered "Other", please identify the point at which your Region assigns an enforcement specialist/civil investigator.					"For removal sites requiring a removal action, an enforcement specialist and civil investigator are assigned as soon as the program determines enforcement is appropriate. At sites that begin as a remedial or Superfund Alternative site, we assign the enforcement specialist and civil investigator when we begin the PRP search."				"For some sites Region 9 assigns enforcement personnel during the removal phase."	
19.	At what point in an NPL site's life-cycle does your Region assign an attorney to the site?	"Attorneys are usually assigned to a site when the initial PRP search report is drafted, which usually occurs early on in the process before proposal. They can also be assigned earlier or later depending on the circumstances."					"Attorneys are generally assigned to sites when the initial PRP Search report (Enforcement First Report) is drafted which usually occurs 3 to 6 months before proposal. Attorneys can be assigned earlier or later, depending on circumstances				"It varies but usually during PA/SI Phase. It varies by: complexity of the site, whether or not there are PRPs, if the site began as a removal."

Organization	Region 1	Region 2	Region 3	Region 4	Region 5	Region 6	Region 7	Region 8	Region 9	Region 10
						at the site, workload, etc."				
PA/SI Phase	X			X			X			X
HRS QA			X						X	
NPL Proposal								X	X	
NPL Final										
Post-RI/FS Start										
Post-RA Start										
Other					X				X	
If you answered "Other", please identify the point at which your Region assigns an attorney.					"When we begin preparing the first 104(e) letter."				"For some sites Region 9 assigns an attorney during the removal phase."	
Notes:	Region 1 left several questions unanswered as unknown and was very ambiguous about the assignment of an attorney question (#19). Would recommend follow-up call.	Did not actually complete the survey. Most of it is blank.				Region 6 did provide attachments to their Questionnaire in support of their answers.				Emphasis in statements in the original from the Region.

10

www.ingramcontent.com/pod-product-compliance
Lightning Source LLC
Chambersburg PA
CBHW081739170526
45167CB00009B/3874